light scribbles
from a nomad heart

Adriana Sjan Bijman

Contents

Foreword

Adriana was a Findhorn community member and a resident of Scotland for two decades. Much travelled from her childhood home in the Netherlands, both in Europe and beyond, developing her artistic call and response in France, Italy, Germany, India, the former Soviet Union and latterly in Argentina, she eventually chose to make her home in Findhorn; having first visited in 1991, she returned permanently in 1997. The beauty of the Caledonian landscape became her muse. Her study of landscape in its many forms and guises is at once both intimate and empathic.

She was known as a fervent gardener (her own phrase), a chronicler of community life, an illustrator, graphic designer, photographer, blogger, card maker, activist, holder of meditation, and more. Her creative genius found its clearest expression in her writing and in her photoart. It was a conscious decision of hers to publish stories in English, even though her notes are in Dutch as well and Spanish on occasions. She was fiercely proud of her status as a Scottish resident.

Adriana explored and documented her soul's journey through a camera lens (or many lenses) and through the lens of her own experience. She looked at life full in the face, unswervingly, with humour and with courage. She was never afraid to look again, or to try harder, or to accept another challenge. As her eyesight deteriorated and she couldn't use her cameras, she never complained; she found a renewed creative outlet in her writing. The *light scribbles* of her blog took on greater significance, demanding more attention, taking more effort; 'sometimes I wake up and a story is asking to be written down'. This book illustrates that soul's inner journey, its glory and its suffering, from her childhood struggle for identity to the conscious search for connection as an adult and complex woman. And, as she promised, it starts and ends with flowers.

This collection of Adriana's *light scribbles* illustrates the extraordinary archetypal quality of her writing as well as demonstrating an unique and deepening perception of love and light and of life forms. It has a special poignancy in that it represents her last work; she continued to work on it, making design decisions, matching photographs to stories, planning its release, until she died in April 2017. She wanted it to be beautiful and it is. She thought it might be her last work, and it is.

Thank you, beloved.

Pat Ellison, Forres

April 2018

Introduction

I am not a writer. I don't have a regular writing practice. The stories come irregularly, as little gifts or presents to be unwrapped. Sometimes to accompany a photo, sometimes separately.

This is a collection of photos and stories made in different styles, over the last nine years. Different photography styles. Older, very sharp black and white pictures, the rest in colour, in focus or, on purpose, created in movement – arty or amateur, as if I cannot make sharp pictures. Don't worry, I can, very well! I sometimes just prefer not to show my world as a sharp 1/125th of a second of reality. Everything is always changing, moving and re-creating itself. Like we are. Maybe there is a deeper meaning why at the end of 2015 I got distorted eyesight; I was diagnosed with partial sight and, with this nystagmus, could only see the world as a double exposure. Since then, I can only read with difficulty, so I wanted to finish these stories and publish this book before my eyes got worse. But of course, I hope they'll get better instead.

Adriana (Sjan) Bijman, 2017

This book is not about

Photography has been a life-long passion, outlasting any special relationship, sometimes competing with it, but always winning in the end, although not always without pain. I also loved text, writing. I have had an education as a graphic designer at the Gerrit Rietveld Kunstacademie in Amsterdam, as I sensed that the kind of photography I'd like to practise would not make me a good living. Loving forms, colours and design, graphic design seemed a logical choice.

As a young girl, the local windowsills had fascinated me and I longed to design as an adult. Or I wanted to take over the local newspaper and printer's, and do interviewing, writing and printing. I once created a small newsletter for our farming hamlet I grew up in. Later, as an adult, there came a stream of posters, magazines, LP then CD and DVD-covers, as well as my own books and photo-art series. And during my last academic year in 1982, I worked at the oldest, still-existing Dutch daily newspaper Het Haarlems Dagblad as photo-editor, and in 1992 as a journalist, sharpening my pen at a press agency in the north.

As a young girl of about 12, I dreamed of being able to speak French, to live in France and in a street. Then I forgot about it. Until, at the age of 20, I found myself having realised this longing. In the youth hostel, we worked in an international residential team. The photographer from Quebec taught me how to develop my films. The Japanese guy imported a whole range of professional (still analogue) Olympus lenses and cameras for me. I had to pick them up in Switzerland, duty-free. At the border, they were not interested in my illegally-imported cameras as they held me for several hours, in search of hidden drugs; being Dutch and bathed

in patchouli oil, I was bound to make any customs officer suspicious back then. Of course, they were right, but they didn't find any proof.

The youth hostel was my first experience of living and working together, as a kind of small community.

I tried to repeat this experience in different ways, in 'woonwerkgemeenschappen', until I visited Findhorn for the first time in 1991. I had heard about its 30 years of being a community, but did not know anything about its spiritual basis. But then and there in 1991, I knew I would come back to live there. First though, I had to warm up my bones and find some peace with Eileen's Christian guidances. In the south of Germany, in Stuttgart, the city of Rudolf Steiner, in Baden-Würtemberg I lived, worked and enjoyed four warm summers, as well as starting a spiritual search. At Christmas 1997, I came back to Findhorn for silent retreat, and it called me to make the move to this remote community on the Scottish north coast. And I have been here ever since.

The texts and photos in this book do not tell the story of my life in the Dutch women's movement in the 70s and 80s, when I lived in Haarlem in the Netherlands. Where I lived with some lesbian friends in a house together, or earlier above the printer's Het Drukhuis, where we, as a small collective, helped organisations and individuals from the whole left-wing local world to spread word of their political ideas and actions. As well as our own ones. The book Wilde Haren (1977, De Vrieseborch) uses words and photos to tell about women of those decades.

This book does not contain my personal history in the Haarlem squat movement. The best time I had then was living in a former spice and vinegar factory, HaasKühne, in the Spaarnwouderstraat. I remember the smell of eastern spices hanging over the banks of river Spaarne.

Then there were, what I call, the Italian years, in the 80s, in which I frequently lingered for months for love in Firenze and in Venezia, where new friends lived. I travelled along the coasts of Italy by train, cruised to Palermo in its most southern point. I had learned Italian and my best graphic-art work of these years was the photo-collage series Pronto Per Partire ("dai, dai vieni a Palermo") in large silk-screened black and white prints and a sound-slide show. And the Italian cimiteri (graveyards), like at Isola di San Michele in the lagoon of Venice, I endlessly photographed to add to my life-long, sometimes obsessive, photo-archive of cemeteries. How we as people treat our deaths tells something about how we stand in life. And religion pops in. During travels in the former Soviet Union, I discovered the enormous differences between the isolated, flooded cemeteries outside Moscow in the Perestroika time of President Gorbatsjov, and, at the other side of the communist territory, in the Georgian capital Tbilisi, the abundant graveside lunch parties with music and singing held by family and friends on anniversaries. The discreetly-covered small headstones in parks in California compared with the abundant Black Madonna honouring in Mexico.

Neither does this book tell the story of my Veenkoloniën years (1988-1995) in the northern Dutch province of Groningen. After two years of diving in its history and its contemporary agriculture, I published the results of a governmental photo commission with Veenkoloniaal Verlangen. It had awoken my love for the region and I moved up here, from Haarlem, and settled in a small house with a huge horse chestnut tree along one of the traditional canals on the moor at Kiel-Windeweer. Op Goede Gronden (about eco-farming) and Female Farmers, were amongst my exhibited large photo projects of that time. Ten years later, in 1998, I self-published a book about this unique village and life in the countryside In Kiel-Windeweer bladert de wind door de tijd. Photos with poetic texts from interviews with villagers, as well from historical places. I remember making the text corrections in Findhorn, during a three-month programme LCG (Living in Community Guest), working in the garden as my service department.

I have been a fervent traveller, and you'll see stories and photos from some of those travels. Probably the travelling, nourishing the nomad in me, prepared me for all the moving and even becoming homeless. I worked on this book during the last year from five different home addresses.

As they say: Home is inside us.

Forres, 2016

Flowering-rush (Zwanebloemen, Butomus umbellatus) along channel, Dorregeester polder, 2007

Tea Time, Hay Time

Songs were in my head, and I hummed them aloud in parts, a bit like the birds landing and taking off from the dry, recently-mowed pastures. Warm sunshine on the red silk in my dark, ponytail hair.

I was not just walking on the polder path. I was on a mission. I did not let myself get distracted by the bright yellow dotters (buttercups) and blue vergeet-mij-nietjes (forget-me-nots) along the way. I knew the men were all looking forward to seeing me coming. Until they did, they would not stop turning over the dried grass from one row into another with their large wooden hay rakes. Other men would not stop raking those rows together to heaps. And the strongest men of our neighbourhood would not stop lifting the dry loads of hay onto the wooden cart. Making hay while the sun shines. One man on top of the pile would take the dried grass lifted up to him, and put it skilfully into place on the cart, to pack in as much of the future's fodder as possible. They would be sweaty, drips dropping into large wet patches on their open white shirts leaving large spots. Some would be naked to the waist.

My shoulders started to hurt. It was massive, what I was carrying. The thermos flask with sweet milk coffee; the many, many bottles of malt beer; the packages with speculaas-cookies and Marie-biscuits.

Tired from the strain of work, we would all sigh deeply and roll ourselves into a row along a large hay heap. We would open the bag and share the drinks and the sweet food. "Bring tea at three," they had said, and someone at home had prepared the big bag for me to bring to the last meadow near the windmill and dyke of our polder. I knew that's where they were haying. I was glad I had not forgotten it. I felt important.

They will give me some beer too, I knew. I do not like it, but I will drink it anyway and make funny faces, and they will all laugh at me and make me laugh too. Maybe they will let me help them and I will come home at our farm high on top of the hay cart. I love that.

I can see them now. I can smell them now.

10 February 2007

Dorregeesterpolder, the Netherlands, 2007

Pinksterblommen

The dairy farmers do not like to see them in their meadows. Pinksterblommen or cuckoo flowers. Lady's Smock. Cardamine pratensis. Flocks of white and pink, pastel lilac rosette flowers in the young grass. I was told their name comes from the Roman Catholic celebration of Pinksteren, Pentecost, Whitsuntide. That's when they blossom. Forty days after Easter. Two Sundays in a row to celebrate. Tourists flooding in from Germany to visit the Dutch polders. The Dorregeester lake with its water sport facilities, its fishing places, its canals and colourful flowery meadows full of the Holland-Frysian black and white cows, which trample on the yellow buttercups and dandelions and graze between the softness of the cuckoo flowers.

In the polders. My father knew all about them. He was a small but successful cow breeder and dairy farmer, and chairman of the polder, which lay far beneath sea level. He was in charge of its water levels and dikes. He told me buttercups and cuckooflowers on your land meant the soil was too acid and poor in minerals. Its grass would become poor cow food. Like the wild flowers growing abundantly on poor sandy roadsides. I listened but liked the colourful carpets between the polder ditches.

We would walk together in silence along the canals to check the water level. If it was too high or too low, he would adjust the floodgates at the large mill. I loved the abundant blue forget-me-nots along our way there and would pick them to take home. In my little corner of the attic, I would decorate my safe haven by filling our new housekeeper's empty bottles of hair conditioner with my wild flower bunches.

Once I held his hand while we walked and we were as close as we ever could be as father and daughter. Not in words, those were never much present. But in releasing our pains to the wind and the water. In our love for the land. In our love for my mother, whom we just had lost unexpectedly. Unable to share the bare wounds, unable to cry, unable to hold me in any other way, but to find comfort in taking a walk together into the meadows. The land, as we would call it. The Zevenmorgen de Vijfmorgen, Grietje Post, plots with ancient names on a rough row along the winding waterside. With birds nesting in patches of long grass. With the group of new born calves, jumping up and down like crazy, testing out their first year's legs, bumping with joy into the gates, into each other. They were there with us. With all the colourful fragrant wild flowers and the young grass that gave the best May cheese. The Beaujolais of the cow's milk cheeses. Life right in our face. Life going on. Even if we wanted it to halt. Even if we desperately wanted to turn back time. Or at least understand what was going on in our confused hearts. In our drowning hearts. In our slaughtered hearts, like still born calves cut into pieces on the cold kitchen table. Wrapped and put into the freezer. Numb.

Let me come home my hands filled with Pinksterblommen.

May 2008

Schiermonnikoog, 2011

Koekoeksbloemen *

Ouch! With bare feet I jump through the wild grassland, and feel the nettles catch me before I can reach the pink flowering plants. I pick one flower so that I can draw it. To look it up in the Wild Flower Key Book I am consulting in these walled gardens of Totleigh Barton. Like the apple blossoms above me and the banging bluebells at the pond, I am sunbathing on this lovely morning. Orchestras of frogs, birds and bees around my little writing haven. But I'm not really relaxed inside. It's a bit of a nuisance not to find the name of the flower in English. I'm just going to give you its Dutch name: Koekoeksbloemen. Maybe that's how we all should call them from now on. Koekoeksbloemen. They bring me right back to the botanical peninsula of Spaarndam, where biologists came to count the bird eggs and determine the flower species. I lived there on a tjalk, a former river transport boat, illegally, as did five other ship owners. The place was a small paradise of flowers and nourished my lifelong love for them. But this was not where I knew the koekoeksbloemen from, I only recognised them. Photographed them. Collected them to dry. Classified them for my first flower books.

They were much older than the 1970s. They went to primary school with me, a nun school, where I once offered a bunch of wild flowers to the teacher. My belief in flowers already was so strong, that I was not thrown off balance when she did not receive them in the way they were given: as a present, a gift of the meadows and roadsides near my home. She threw them in the dustbin with a sneer.

From then on it was clear to me she was stupid and no longer worthy of my admiration. I would teach myself.

What did she know about the meaning of flowers? She did not live in our polder with the endless meadows; the small canals ditches and watersides, the farm orchards with vegetable gardens and wild mysterious spots. I would not tell her the hiding place between the cow stable and the newly built barn with the smell of fresh hay and the big plum tree under which I buried my secret treasures. Where I hid myself to stay away from the new housekeeper who wanted to take my mother's place in the house. She did not see the flocks of daisies (Chrysanthemum leucathemum) around the old pear tree at the Vijfmorgen, like the circle dancers I got to know decades later. What did she know about the taste of the white deadnettle (Lamium album) which we carefully picked from in between the prickling nettles (Urtica dioica) so that we could suck out the nectar? Later, much later, I discovered their taste had changed. Or was it that these plants only offer this treat to children and that as adults we can no longer taste this delicious nectar? Maybe they are a different variety or have environmental pollution and the use of herbicides and pesticides diluted its taste, like it has done with so many of our vegetables? I don't know.

My teacher did not smell the chamomile (Chamaemelum nobile) that crept everywhere. She did not know the wild yarrow (Achillea millefolium). Nor the strong yellow dandelion (Taraxacum officinale), bright as the sunshine itself, the leaves of which I liked to chew. Then I'd spit them out, like I saw the old farmers do with their tobacco, while I wandered between the cows, pretending to inspect them.

But most of all she did not know the koekoeksbloem in my little flower bunches. Their bright magenta pink heads standing out in the meadow like princesses in the crowd. Their now soft stems getting warm in my hands, as I ride my little red bike, the two kilometres from the farm in the Dorregeester polder to the girls' school in the village.

She neither taught us the names of the flowers, nor how they live. She and her colleagues taught us the laws of arithmetic, the capitals of the provinces and the grammatical exceptions of the past tense, things I would listen to, as I was curious. I learned to be quick and clever as a survival tool in the village and later on in town. But this was a different kind of learning from my private discovering of the taste of the white deadnettle blossoms, and the delightful koekoeksbloem.

May 2008

* Silene flos-cuculi or Lychnis flos-cuculi, the native European wild flower Ragged Robin.

Schiermonnikoog, the Netherlands, 2007

Meditation

"I still am not so good at meditating," I confessed to my friend M. Well, at least not indoors. I wish I could find within the sanctuaries of calm peace, deep concentration and connection that I easily feel when I sit in nature. Simply. Silently. Hearing the wind calms and grounds me. Seeing the moss green on a tree bark brings me joy. Flowers seduce me. Feeling the soft spring air nourishes me and fills much more than just my lungs. A bird calls and we both know we are part of something so big, so immense that our thoughts cannot even fly there. But our voices are heard everywhere. Our hearts, our cores are known, even by name.

Not that I learned this at school during the religion classes from the Catholic priest who tried to get us praying and going to daily church services. The nuns-teachers scolded us for not going, but we lived in a farming hamlet in the countryside, far beyond the village. Without breakfast I would faint, and sometimes did so during the Sunday morning Mass.

But praying we also did at home. A 'Holy Father' before and after a meal, and more after breakfast. All of us on our knees in front of our chairs. Each of us taking their turn in praying, or mumbling one of the prayers of Hope, Faith and Love or one of the Hail Marys in between. Not appreciating the meaning of the words, because we had never learned them or were too young to understand, or because we could not connect with them in our own lives. My father started the praying with a 'Holy Father', after which came we children, one after the other. Each hurting our young, tender knees and hearts, longing to hear the absent female leading voice. A void we did not know how to fill. Like the rearrangement of chairs around the table, which only showed something was wrong. We did not get used to it. We made our prayers fray, gabbling them as quickly as we could, knowing that our friends were waiting for us outside, or even inside, awkwardly standing at the kitchen door. Eager to jump on our bikes to school some kilometres away from our polder hamlet, away from the painful atmosphere in the farm kitchen.

Walking through the polder though was different. It was special. Alone, or sometimes with my father, who took me with him to check the water level of the canals in our polder, before adjusting it at the mill. The calm green rippling meadows of the polder. Wide and spacious, or dotted with black and white cows and wild herbs. Canals with reed and colourful flowers along the banks of rippling water. Sounds of frogs and birds. A breeze through my hair. No talking. Sometimes a hand held.

Through this I learned my way of praying, meditating, being. My nature-meditation.

Findhorn, 8 March 2016

Washing the price winning cow, Dorregeest, 2012

A 100,000 litre cow

During the second world war, my father bought a cow, a traditional black and white Holland-Frysian Stamboekvee cow called Hoekstra 6, with which he and my mother started a dairy farm at Dorregeest in one of the old Dutch polders. Hoekstra 6 became the matriarch of a long line of dairy cows on the farm. The Hoekstras received many awards, their bull calves became famous for their semen and many Hoekstras were sold worldwide. This June my brother and sister-in-law, who live on the parental farm, had a party for Hoekstra 545, one of their 100,000 litre milk cows.

During her career of 13 years the celebrated cow gave 11 calves and 100,000 litres of milk.

November 2012

There were Poems

There were poems

Written on my lips

Which were as leaves as pages – to leaf through

And they were many

Soft and rounded

As rose petals

Opening around their core

On a Sunday, the 13th of June

French rose, 2009

Shadow and Light

This image pops up every now and then in my photo-archive. I love its simplicity: the little shadowed meadow with the light reflection of the window on it.

There was more to it though. I made this picture when I was very ill, lying in bed for months, facing big questions like: 'Can I still see the light when I seem to be surrounded by shadow?' and 'Can I say 'Yes' to life, when death is luring?' I did answer 'Yes', to the fullest, and recovered. My neighbour, who could see the same meadow from the other side, committed suicide.

Findhorn, 2004

The Park Findhorn, 2004

Liebesangst *

It was only on the last day that we kissed each other. Not just the three continental kisses on the cheeks, nor the brief touch of lips, of the last decades. This was crossing the border. This was real kissing. Lips that dare to open, tongues that tinglingly explore the valleys and caves of the mouth. Tongues losing time in tasting each other. Find time. Find place. Our tongues seemed to take over the town.

We had spent five days together in her home and in her hometown Berlin. As a tour guide she showed me the historical places, explained the political reasons, the social content of every street we crossed; of every building I laid my eyes on. Serious. Deep. I would not start. I would not seduce her. I would not kiss her full lips, her joyful large blue eyes, her curly soft hair, her straight shoulders, or her single breast. Imagining she too longed for it.

Twenty-five years earlier she had lived on her own for a week in my room in Haarlem, while I had fallen in love with Morocco. The Medina near the desert, with its endless red sands, dust and heat had entered my skin. And my heart. I was in love and my Moorish blood – woken up – took over the reins in my veins. The body became precious earth longing to express its love.

I slowly came back and saw her sitting in the corner of my eyes. She placed herself in front of me and as talking to her reflection in a mirror, she asked, "And when do we kiss?" I cherished her beautiful question over the years. I do not remember the answer. Did we ever then?

Changing and rearranging the memory of the stories of the heart. Sejerø, 30 years ago. Once we stayed on the Dutch island of Texel in a remote beach hut. We quarrelled and I sent her away, or she left, and I claimed the hut as my work studio. What happened between the two women we were then? Can you tell me about the mystery of love? Can you explain the stories of fear? Why are we smitten by one person and another gives us the shivers? A fear carefully keeping us at a distance. When is fear a healthy answer to the red warning signs of our internal traffic lights, and when it is an old Trojan horse full of misleading, unprocessed childhood patterns? And how can we be sure which one it is?

I think she, the tour guide, led us and in the safety of our mouths I followed, blindfolded, trusting, despite the fear.

Berlin-Findhorn, January 2008

* Fear of love

It was only on the last day, that we kissed each other. Not just three continental kisses on the cheeks. Not the very quick touch of lips, as we had done over the last decades. This was crossing the border. This was real kissing. Lips which open, tongues which tingling explore the valleys and caves of the mouth. Tongues that taste each other and loose time. Find time. Find place. Our tongues seemed to take over the town.

Berlin, 2008

Light Written

The Light written on the walls
Her presence coming into
This morning

England, Totleigh Barton, Beaworthy, May 2008

Totleigh Barton, Beaworthy, 2008

I found Her like this

I found her like this
Her body trusting like a young girl.
I took her in
slowly skin hair soft
shining like worn silk.
Every wrinkle a line my fingers imagine walking into
memories of a woman's life lived
and maybe I am that age too.
I wonder
how will it feel – to be the one who knows her.
 The one she longs for
in her sleep

I found her like this

Findhorn, 3 August 2008

Findhorn dunes, 2008

Growing Light

While I wake up

after that night, you know which one I mean

I touch the breathtaking light growing into a new day

into my heart

and wonder

how long it will stay

or how quickly it will fade away

I wonder

how long I can let it stay

and if I can let go while it moves again, away

Mallorca, April 2011

Mallorca, 2011

How precious it is to be human

One night I dreamed I had two children, whom I loved so totally and unconditionally that the remembrance of that love in the dream completely nourished me in the daytime world.

I felt loved too and did not take life and love for granted.

How rare and precious it is to be human, not because it is better than other life forms, but because we have the amazing capacity to make choices.

Findhorn, 12 September 2011

Barcelona, Spain, 2007

Blues & Greens

Blues
were always your favourite,
your eyes, your moods too.
I borrowed yellow
from the Pachamama's sun
to guide us into the greens

Greens
In the green we met.
Olive groves a thousand years old
holding our young embrace
in tenderly touching branches.
They know about time.
We had not met yet.

2011

Blue cornflowers in green (Centaurea), (on new film) , Findhorn

I bike home

I bike home

I fold the laundry

I peel the potatoes and cut the kale

I wash a pullover and hang it out to dry

I put the laundry away

I cook the 'stamppot' with some salt and oat flakes

I fry an egg with it

I clear the dishes of this morning's breakfast

when I did not know yet

my lover has left me.

Findhorn, 2012

Isle of Skye, Scotland, 2008

Holding on to the Light

Discoloured wallpaper
In hand-painted floral patterns on
Layers of wealth – unwelcome now – and dust of decades
Covering the secrets and scars of the past,
Suddenly illuminated
And my eyes, desperately trying to hold on to the light. Slowly then
Our chances fade again.
We were blind anyway
Not opening our windows.

Buenos Aires/Findhorn, spring 2013

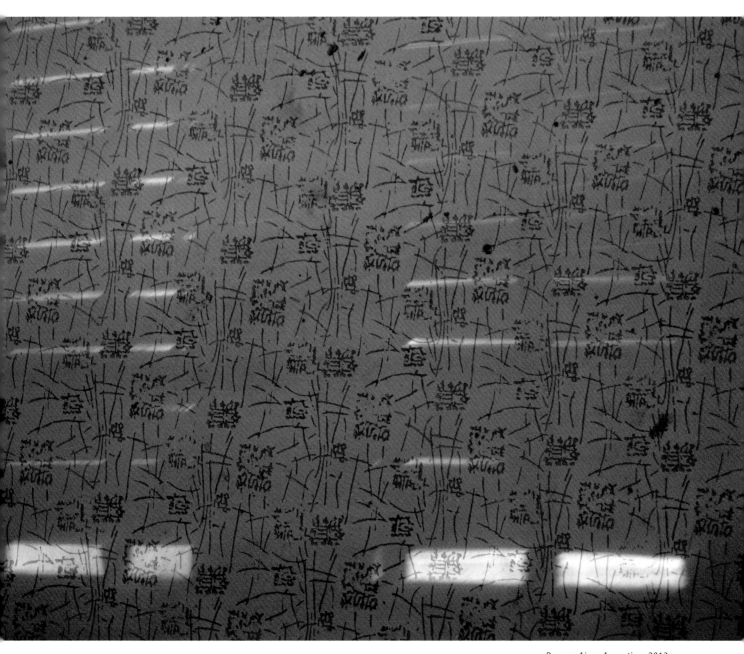

Buenos Aires, Argentina, 2013

You think you know me

You think you know me
because you know how to give me names
that hold me in the past
but are unknown to the poetry that feeds me
and ignorant of the stories in my heart
which wait to be narrated
in a new tongue
in other words
     we can create new books
     written and bound by hand – if we choose
     in which
     I maybe might know you
     if I give you back your real name

At the end of the noughties

Selfportrait (one of the many!), Iona, 2014

Our Soul's Longing

Last week, while the Findhorn Birthday Book proof prints were being produced, I went to the Netherlands for six days, to visit two friends whom I have known for more than 35 years. They don't know each other, but, oddly enough, in January both were told they had terminal cancer, and had only two months to live. I held them in my meditations and prayers at the Sunday morning Healing meditation. Both of them told me they were not ready to leave this planet, yet. They would definitely wait for me to visit. And they did.

It was moving, and a great joy, to see them and connect deeply again. But what so surprised and interested me was the very different ways in which each of them chose to fill these last months of their lives. I thought that was incredible.

H, a well-known photographer, decided to organise and scan his whole analogue photo-archive and leave good prints for his family to sell, so ensuring an income for them in the coming years. He printed a whole new, amazingly beautiful, series of tulips pictures, and made it into a portfolio. It was so inspiring and joyful to sit together and share our love for nature and our 'life-task' of bringing this love forth through photography.

Then I visited my friend I, who had decided to do the complete opposite. She had released all her work, volunteering projects and social obligations, and went totally inwards, to prepare herself for this upcoming new big journey. She had organised a big day-long Buddhist-inspired meditation with all her friends to release them and they her, and to all reflect and do the inner work on their attachments.

Both of my friends were living to the fullest during these months; more than they ever thought possible. I came back fulfilled and inspired, sure that they both were, and are, answering their soul's longing, purpose and goal of being here in this life; at this time, in this place.

This was a big example to me that we never know how long we will be here for. I got the message to set priorities and put the most important ones first, not somewhere 'in ten years' at place number six. No, now, at number one.

Thank you for being here.

Findhorn, May 2012

Hallway of former monastery Son Rullan, Mallorca, 2011

Kindertjes (kids), Mooye Nel, near Haarlem, around 1977

No motherhood

A friend wrote to me saying how shocked she was when I had told her that as a child I was very certain that I didn't want to be a mother but instead wanted to dedicate my life to artwork, to follow my passion for colours and drawing. Instead of acquiring a husband and a circle of kids to tend to, as I had seen my own mother doing, I would choose art work as an adult woman.

From an early age, I filled every piece of empty paper available in the house with colouring, drawing, and scribbling. I drew mostly on folio sheets, partly stencilled with minutes from one of the several committee chair functions my father held, alongside being a farmer. When I asked my mother where her drawings were, she said she had destroyed the old ones, and since she had us had given up drawing. At that very young age – a toddler, not at kindergarten yet – I decided this would not happen to me and with stubborn determination I said I did not want to become a mother. The women present laughed. But I knew I wanted to grow up drawing and colouring and all such things. I wanted to use my creativity to the full, if possible make it my profession. I definitely would not become a mother, if it meant stopping drawing. This was the end of the 1950s and there were not many examples nor windows of possibility for women to combine work and motherhood. Family members expected my decision to change as I grew older. I did check it with myself every about five years, but it stayed the same. After my mother died and my favourite housekeeper also left us bundle of kids, to have children of her own, I added another reason. If I some day wanted to be a mother, I would take care of the many already existing children, who are longing with arms held upwards to be loved and cared for. I would adopt them or co-mother a partner's children. And, much later, did so. In adult years I got to understand that human overpopulation on our planet is one of the main reasons for the climate change, bringing worldwide devastating problems of famine and sorrow. I would not add to those numbers.

A woman's decision to choose her creative passion and ambition never received good reviews. You don't have to be much of a feminist to acknowledge the difficulties women had around this in history. Women writers, however famous, still were called spinsters. Is there a male equivalent to blacken him, like calling an unmarried artist a 'spinner'? No, it was normal for a man to answer the deeper call and become a writer, artist or explorer; he could be admired for his choice. Mostly there even would be women (or men) who'd like to be at his side, in his shadow, as a support or muse. For a woman it mostly has been different.

continued on next page

Both my father and mother had six siblings, and all had at least six children. All of my brothers and sister became parents. I was the exception. My whole life I only had short relationships, often ending when I felt I had to choose between the partner and my art work. The latter always won. Not always without pain or guilt.

The guilt women suffer in choosing their heart's desire and ambition, has been passed on for generations, centuries, through the female bloodline in our patriarchal society. So deeply, it became internalized as oppression in ourselves, and the norm.

How I loved to have examples of those who had eschewed motherhood. Imagine a sister of my great-great-grandmother, whose letters with her little drawings would arrive by horse-drawn carriage from the archaeological sites near Pompeii. Imagine an aunt, who made a living from her illustrations, and whose books I secretly leafed through. They were kept in the dresser in the *'opkamer'* the lounge, where we only were allowed to sit on birthdays or during winter, as it was the only heated room in the farmhouse.

For centuries, single women were ridiculed and not taken seriously. Seldom did a woman artist become famous in her time. The Haarlem painter Judith Leijster depicts herself in a famous self-portrait as a self-confident artist. As did the Baroque painter from Rome, Artemisia Gentileschi (1590-1656). She gained great respect and recognition for her work, while the aristocracy gave her commissions. I especially admire her impressive oil painting of the biblical scene Judith slaying Holofernes. But both women artists were exceptions, as often women had to work, write or publish under a man's name in order for their work to be accepted. Happily that has changed.

My decision not to become a mother but to follow the desire and calling from deep within my heart and soul to express myself through creative work, never did change. It has been the most important decision in my life. I have never, not even for a second, regretted this.

Findhorn, April 2016

'Vaas bij Saar', Amsterdam, 1977

Shifting boundaries

One night, I once again dream of death; a repeating theme lately. I am waiting for several people to die, and they seem to take ages to do so. Slowly, they slowly turn into brownish-grey mud beings. I stand aside, witnessing it, left desolate.

It reminds me of a sentence I once read, "Now, in the middle of the journey of my illness, I am left alone and defenceless."(1)

A realisation pops up that the dying people are part of me; the old me, from whom I want to detach, release or transform. As I am not totally ready to do so, in the dream I feel an uncomfortable sense of guilt towards them, as if I am betraying them. Letting them die seems as if they were not good enough, as if the old me maybe was not good enough? I have to tell them that they were, at the time, but that now I no longer need what they stand for: qualities of my pre-illness past, like impatience, direct sharp communication, and the multi-tasking workaholism. Let those qualities serve other people now.

Time for some housework it seems, as I then dream I am being forced into a gloomy cellar to clean the incredibly filthy steps descending before me; a horrible task I have been given to undertake. Finally, after finishing it, I discover an old squeaking door in the cellar, which brings in fresh air and light. What a relief!

My old organisational skills are well placed to open new doors, I think. I would like to invite and integrate a new me, new personalities, as a gift on this journey of illness. Dissimilar to the old me in many ways. Not only physically older, but also wiser, with more experience on the inner. This physical condition teaches me new boundaries to what I can do, and can no longer. At other times, it forces me even to give up all limits and borders, depending on the shifting sands of my energy. It teaches me compassion, patience and slowing down, in fact a lot of slowing down. Taking this in, I realise I now want to live with a matured set of boundaries, whether I am ill or healthy.

(1) from The Alchemy of Illness, 1993, by Kat Duff

Findhorn, February 2016

Fences at agriculture land on the isle of Skye, 2008

Illness: Dark & light

I am living in the twilight, in the middle of a journey. The door of the past, with its healthy body in a very busy life, has been closed and it is not clear where the road will take me.

"Illness is a simple though painful reminder that we are not the masters of our bodies and our lives,"(1) writes Kat Duff. Illness is a humbling experience, and, as such, I think can bring some gifts in disguise. Insights wrapped up as setbacks in the Game of Life.

After seven months of gradually increasing symptoms, discomfort and pains, instead of a slow or quick recovery, I am having to accept and learn to live with this long term illness, like many people do. It has turned my life upside down, thrown me out of my comfort zone and the fulfilment of a hardworking busy life. It makes me stand apart, in another category, that of the ill, the weak, the elderly, the non-productive. It is a different journey. It feels like that, even here, in a community based on a spiritual life; most people always seem to be so busy and often are on the edge of being burned out, trying to do so well, to save the world or at least save our community. Or simply trying to earn a living so that they can control the ongoing stream of bills. Like I did over the last decades.

At first this big change brought up feelings of tension, guilt and questioning, "Why me?" Feeling a bit of a victim. At times I even blamed myself for my illness, from the point of view of certain schools of psychology, that state that 'with our thoughts we create our own reality'. So why did I create this? And why can't I now immediately create a healthy body?

It is easy to stumble into the pitfall of self-blame and being responsible for illness ourselves. These thoughts are absolutely not helpful to me now. It does not mean I am not willing to look at a deeper personal cause of what my body is doing and how I can help to get out of this predicament; how to make my journey towards a better life. How I can make peace with the symptoms. How we can become allies instead of enemies and how we can start to work together for the same goal. For me, a goal of balance.

Since I was a young girl, my whole life has been an experience of learning how to have and maintain independence. Although I now know we all are inter-dependent, it is a tough journey to learn to ask for help. I can already feel grateful for and see the advantages of newly-learned qualities like patience and slowing down. The 'being dependent' and compassion are in progress, so to speak. I've always been a multi-tasker, a quick thinker and doer. Slowing down, especially to prevent more accidents with my vertigo-dizziness and only partial eyesight, makes me clumsy. I walk like a drunken sailor on land. Out of doors with crutches, for my own safety. Constantly having to balance myself is exhausting, but also contains the lesson of balancing the way of life. How to bring more balance into my, our lives? How to bring some light in the darkness? The light of keeping up my spirit, my hope, my goals of renewed good health.

Simple, but at times exhausting, survival activities like washing, getting dressed, shopping nearby and cooking, easily fill my days, along with time to rest. "How did I ever have time to work?" I grin and wonder. Too tired to pick up a pen or pencil during the daytime, texts like this only come in the sleepless dark hours of the night, scribbled on and in between the lines, which I can hardly distinguish. It does not matter: I recognised the words and pass them on to you here, as part of my journey. Like during the winter season here, I am on my way to more light.

(1) The Alchemy of Illness, 1993, by Kat Duff

Forres, December 2015

Scottish landscape along the north-east coast, December 2015

Lake los Andes, Chile, 2009

El Tronador

The last eight kilometres towards the sacred mountain is a tough track where water and wind rule. We leave the twisting Rio Negro behind us. All along the road the colihue, tall green bamboo, the native caña bows and bounces back. The native Indians used it for fishing in the seven coloured glacier lakes and for hunting. It has a life cycle of about 50 years. After it flowers it goes into seed and dies. The seeds eaten by mice and birds acts as a pest control, exploding in their stomachs and killing them. Diego, the tour guide on this trip through Patagonia, calls it 'a natural death'.

The native tribes, the Tehuenche, who had a secret track through the Andes, used this method to get rid of the new intruders here, the Jesuits, in the 17th century. The Jesuits had discovered this track, which gets you through the Andes into Chile in only three days, instead of the long track of 20 to 30 days the Spanish used to take. After a filling meal with a local tribe all the Jesuits died 'a natural death' and the secret of the path was saved for another 100 years.

But today we are driving on it. The natives lost their secret, and much more than that besides. Nowadays the trail is part of the national park Nahuel Huapi. But this still is the track to the sacred mountain, El Tronador, the thunderer. The ancients believed this mountain range housed a spirit, which would roar in anger from time to time, leaving tremendous sounds and shakings echoing through the valleys, causing the the ice of the glaciers to move. It was forbidden to climb these mountains.

Our path meanders through an endless green forest. Bamboo and other trees are covered with 'old men's beard', hanging moss-green lichen; signs of the unusally clean air. During one stop, I sit between lichen-covered branches in a silent enchanting valley, when at a distance a noise and a troupe of slim brown horses appear galloping on a thin track in the dense, fogged forest. After a while a horse with driver come into view, wool and leather around the man. It could be a Mapuche or Tehueche, hunting one of the small resilient Patagonian deer that has lived here for millennia, or being hunted by a puma.

Once el Tronador was a volcano, million of years ago, and its lava fertilized the whole area. After that, the massive glaciers rolled and roared through the mountains leaving valleys and lakes. Millennia later, melting ice filled them with water carrying minerals and sediments, which coloured the lakes. At the foot of el Tronador unfolds a black glacier surrounded by milk-turquoise partly frozen glacier water. Over the recent decennia this immense ice valley has started to melt. We are shown the tree line where, 30 years ago, the ice could be touched, but now it is lying in a new valley. If climate change continues its effects as quickly as it does now, all of the black ice might end up as a new lake in a couple of years.

El Tronador itself, a row of mighty mountains, keeps itself hidden in the clouds today. We cannot see the tops of its immense heights. Earlier this year, after a heavy rainfall, a part of the glacier broke off and caused an avalanche in the wide surroundings. We see complete 25 metre-high trees that were split like matches. The water's destroying brute force has left bare land where once a forest existed. One giant rock, I guess three metres high, has rolled down the mountain side, as if God or the Spirit of el Tronador has been playing bowling. Cruel. Torn open earth. Leaving a wounded hill.

And el Tronador still roars. From afar, and I hope a safe distance, while admiring its black glacier under a pouring sky, I suddenly hear its thundering sounds, again and again. Then its echo in the valleys.

I say my prayer to the ancient volcano spirit, el Tronador.

Patagonia, Argentina, 27 October 2009

Torres de Paine, Chile, 2009

Travel notes from El Calafate

Imagine the glorious view the original Indian pueblo, the Tehuelche, must have beheld when they entered this valley where the stream descends between the snowy mountains near the glaciers. Its hills filled with the bright yellow blossoms of the low green prickly shrubs, later in the season giving its purple nourishing berries, would be such a good change from their diet of guanaco. This herd animal, a wild relative of the Andes llama, gave them their meat, its soft fleece clothed them, and its leather covered the roofs of their huts.

I imagine they stopped their nomadic life for a while to stay at the gentle stream in the flat, green area between the mountains at the laguna or small lake. I can see it happening.

But it happened much earlier of course. Millennia earlier, during the ice age, the glaciers flowed down to here, and when the ice melted, it left behind the lagunas in the valley, the strangely shaped rock, volcanic and metamorphic, while the strong winds blew in the slow growing lichen and algae. Then followed the tough pampas grass called coidones, and much later, to grow between its clumps, came the prickly evergreen plants calafate, the Berberis buxifolid.

The life of the Indian nomads was turned upside down by invaders, Spanish explorers coming from another world. The newcomers took the wool of the sheep, transporting it overland for 350km to the Atlantic coast. They too made a resting place at the same stream at the laguna amongst the snowy mountains, founding the settlement of El Calefate. They brought their own sheep. The Tehuelche, who did not understand the domestication of animals, hunted the sheep and were later on hunted themselves in an expedition to Patagonia at the end of the 19th century. The armed governmental forces killed most of the large native Indian population in a massacre. But a small community of their descendants still survives near the village of El Calafate, one of them tells me.

The purple berry bush is called el Calafate. It is the name of the tourist village at the crossing runways of an airport. This is still a resting place amidst the immensity of the surrounding wild nature, although nowadays for the modern traveler and tourist. They bring an extra income for the large estancias, whose cows, horses and sheep graze on thousands of hectares of bare, poor land. In a truck we ride through a livestock farm called Cerro Huylieche, 22,000 hectares for 600 cows and 150 horses. Another, La Anita encompasses 80,000 hectares.

"There is only 300mm rain per year", the farmer tells us. "The land is bare and it takes four hectares to feed one cow." There are very few guanacos now, so they are protected and have free grazing everywhere. We see Patagonian hares and lots of birds. Los Condores de los Andes pasan, the Andean condor, as well as flamingos, fly above us.

As the snow melts, the land and the tracks become wet and our truck rides through snow and streams in deep mud. The snow chains are put on the 4x4WD truck and I think our driver rides an adventurous daring ride. He is used to it.

I start to connect with this country, learning about its history, its people, and most of all the land, this millennia old Madre Tierra, the Pachamama. I am impressed. I am in love. I kiss the land and the immense rocks make me cry.

It is said that once you have eaten the berry of the Calafate, your return to Patagonia is guaranteed.

(I returned in 2010)
El Calafate, Patagonia, Argentina, 2009-2015

La Garganta del Diablo

A full moon shines over the subtropical humid forest of Iguazú. It is the last night of October: Samhain. Anything can happen as this is a magical time. The Celts knew this, and so did the indigenous people of these South American mountains and green forests. In the middle of these immense wild woodlands – hidden from the European invaders, the conquistadores – are the waterfalls of Iguazú, central to the lives of the Guaraní people for thousands of years. I-guazú, The Great Waters, 21 square kilometres of waterfalls. And in them is the spectacular, powerful La Garganta del Diablo, in Spanish, or Devil's Throat.

After two full days there, I appreciate why no one who ever tried to pass beyond the waterfall came back. Every attempt to construct a bridge has failed, even now our modern technology cannot bridge it. This place of power, beauty and destruction is one of the greatest wonders of our planet. Looking down on hundreds of metres of speeding tons of water, cascading to the left, right, behind, under and on top of us, it is easy to lose all sense, and, at the same time, be only senses.

In the myths of many cultures, the maiden is imprisoned in the underworld for part of the year and only a special act can return her, totally transformed, to this world.

For the Guaraní, the Spirit of the Great Waters took on the shape of a giant serpent. Once a year, they sacrificed a young maiden, a virgin, to the Serpent Spirit, to ensure a good harvest of its fish and fruits. I regularly have come across the meaning of a 'virgin' as a woman who is of her self, not owned by a man. And it is she who is transformed.

I am in no longer a young woman, neither a virgin in the modern sense. But I am a woman wanting to 'own herself' and willing to offer her self for a good cause, and be transformed into a new Self.

I am a Scorpio, a water sign, born in the year of the snake or serpent. This year Saturn returns for a second time to its birthplace in my natal chart. 56 is my initiation year into the Crone. This journey calls for transformation. Time to meet my own Kali in all her shadow and power. What can give more power than this surrendering?

The moon above us is becoming full. This is the time to step forward. Kali wants her offering for this year. There is no choice in choosing to do my own Devil's jump. So I join some South American women leaving in a boat to enter into the Garganta. I will overcome my fear of heights, my fear of water. I step over fear itself as we speed directly into the waterfall. There is no turning back. Then there is one catarata after the other salto, thundering from above, surrounding us, churning below us in an indescribable brutal force of nature. Its vapours spraying upwards, stronger than pouring rain, feel like pure life itself. Standing in awe under the falls I can only surrender, open up and become like water. Honouring the face of Kali.

We become part of the I-guazú. While we scream, while we yell, while we cry, our arms wide open, our hearts torn open, receiving the Spirit of The Serpent of the Great Waters as it receives us, takes us, holds us, until we ourselves become one with Her, and indeed she is Kali herself.

We return to land, exhausted, soaked as if drowned or shipwrecked, but miraculously alive. Here I am, a woman of Her Self, transformed now, reborn through the Great Water.

31 October 2009, Iguazú, Argentina

Cataratas de Iguazú, Argentina/Brasil, 2009

El Sendero Macuco

This is the trail of the yellow butterflies. This is a trail of green wilderness, of nature's perfect chaos in the jungle of the Iguazú. Today I have half price entrance to the Catarátas National Park of Iguazú. Today I'll explore. Without a guide, without a timetable, without plans. After breakfast I take the colectivo, the bus El Preferido to the waterfalls. Yesterday my tour guide Gabriel mentioned something about a walking trail around here and he assured me, "You'll like it". Early morning, as the day opens itself to the already hot sunshine, I start along a small track. Immediately the atmosphere changes, as if a door just closed behind me. Blue flowering shrubs edge a marsh. A buzz is in the air. Carefully I walk into this other world, listening, looking, sensing. With every step I feel my heart opening wider to the joy that seems to breathe here.

The jungle. Green. Wild. Rough. Abundant. A simple path seems to lead to the sound of the water, heading towards one of the many falls. This one is called Salto Arrechea. On the way there I am surprised by the plentiful presence of pink, black and blue mushrooms.

Twisted stems, twin trees. Varieties of bamboo abound, like the gracefully arching Tacuapí or the towering, 20 metre high Tacuarazú. Palm trees. I recognise the Palmito with its delicate edible heart I read about. Protected now, it can only be grown sustainably. Here its elegant presence is unthreatened, between fast-growing shrubs and hundreds of parasitic or symbiotic climbing plants trying to reach the limited open sky. I recognise some from their smaller houseplant versions in our European homes. Here they are lingering and whirling around trunks dozen metres high. For hours I walk in-between and over curling roots that host and water other plants in small water pools after last week's heavy rains.

Bright coloured Toco Toucans, small monkeys, and hundreds of birds in a cacophony of sound, make the music of the forest, competing only with the wind rustling through the dense foliage. Under the red ochre earth and the layers of leaves, geckos, insects and reptiles move or freeze for a moment as we both hold our breath.

Walking on the muddy small trail, I imagine the native American Indians, the Guaraní people, making their way through these high dense green forests, creating the trails before me. After the Guaraní came the early explorers, the conquistadores and colonists. Nowadays these paths are trodden by nature loving hikers like myself, in search for the not so regular tourist trail.

As in most jungles, there is a shortage of salt for all animals. While walking the rough path, I am regularly surrounded by insects, attracted to the sweat on my bare skin, like bees to honey. Some are more welcome than others and I am a bit worried what the insect repellent will do to them. Mosquitoes, flies, but most of all I wonder about the many butterflies. And they come bountifully. Yellow with black colouring, large blue and green ones. Playfully whirling with each other, and, it seems around me. We go forward together. They take it in turns to land on my arm or hand. I stop in admiration. I witness close up their long beaks sucking up the sweat from the pores of my skin. As they sit there, I cherish and enjoy their beauty and trust, in absolute bliss.

1 November 2009, Iguazú. Argentina/Brazil

Butterfly at the Sendero Macuco, Iguazú 2009

La Esperita area, Delta, province of Buenos Aires, 2010

Walking on Water

The Delta is immense. Early mornings, the gentle sound of the water called me and I took a long walk, starting along the river Esperita. I walked and walked, turning left, right, along the water, into the forest.

The delta is immense. I got lost amongst the many wooden piers at the waterfront. I got drunk between the fragrance of unknown colourful, tropical flowers, ripe falling juicy oranges and enchanting high bamboos. I walked and walked.

Was I following in footsteps of the native Guarani Indians who lived here long, long before the Spanish explorers came to this area to settle, take, and kill the Indians? Or were the natives attacked by the Yaguareté, the American jaguar or 'tigre', that lived in the delta and was hunted by the Indian for their beautiful skin and medicinal fat; but which also hunted them? The 'tigre' is not extinct yet…

And then, as I walked my way between the lands, crossing dangerously swaying wooden ways over stream after stream, amidst mosquitos, birds, fish and abundant tropical vegetation, I only could surrender, surrender to become part of everything around me.

And then … then I was walking on water.

Tigre area Delta, Argentina, 2010

In 2010 I visited the delta. From 2011 I exhibited a photo-installation about the walks.

The Delta del Paraná is immense. *It is at the mouth of the second longest river of the world, the Paraná River, which originates in Brazil and meets the sea through the Rio de la Plata at Buenos Aires in Argentina. The widening river splits itself into hundreds of smaller rivers, lingering, searching their way through the dense forest, flooding and creating wetland, marshland and islands. Rivers, streams, creeks and runlets form a network of waterways. They became a vast wild waterscape. The waterways are still the only way to access the whole area. There are bus-boats and taxi-boats to visit the many small islands, which have neither internet nor tap-water nor stabilised electricity. The Tigre delta becomes one again in the River de la Plata (the silver river). Unesco declared a part of the delta region a 'Biosphere natural reserve'. The village at the mouth of the delta carries its name, Tigre. Seen from the sky the delta looks like the skin of the tiger.*

El Teide, Tenerife, Canary Islands, 1996

The devil in 'El Pico del Teide'

For the third time I visited 'el Teide', the most important volcano on the ocean island Tenerife. This time I came from the south of the island, said to have been a desert for millennia. Again El Pico del Teide – the Teide Peak – impressed me with its bare moon-like landscape. The soil seemed fresh erupted black lava of hard rock fragments; on other places the lava was covered with gentle hills of cream coloured sand dust, which was actually volcanic ash, like that which came down from Iceland in 2010, remember? Nothing grows on El Pico. Its earth seems as dead as the native aboriginal people the Guanches, who lived on the islands until the Spanish conquerors arrived at the end of the 15th century. The Guanches believed in the mythology of the Teide and many legends survive, telling us of its divine legacy. It was thought the Teide held the most devilish forces in its crater. Personally I can understand some of that, as a decade ago a superstitious German workshop leader felt drawn to jump into the crater, believing we all would be saved by extraterrestrials. Tenerife is known for its UFO connection. So glad the jump was prevented by the local police!

Nowadays the island lives off the more attractive energies of importing tourists and exporting bananas. You see their poly tunnels everywhere. Like the native Canary Pine tree, the residents have adapted to live off what the land can offer –or they moved away. The abundantly growing pine tree is fire resistant, from blackened trunks they simply rise again into the green. They possess an amazing water-collecting system in their leaves to survive the long periods of drought. It only rains 14 days a year. What a difference from Scotland! We enjoyed the sunshine and warm breezes that cooled down the island. Thank you beautiful island of Tenerife!

May 2014

Cathedral Palma de Mallorca, Easter 2011

'El Teatro de los Sentidos' (Theatre of the senses)

What communicates the impact of light better than this colourful play? It reminds me of the Catalan theatre company Els Comediants, which identifies with the festive spirit of human existence. The goal is not only to open our eyes, but also to be a theatre for the senses. It seems to me that the light in the impressive cathedral in the old city of Palma wants to do just that. There is no separation between the light from the heavens and the space it illuminates. The floor space is like a stage. The stage is the place for the collective experience of the audience, even though we entered as spectators in the house of the Gods. The benches are waiting for the Heathen and Pagan worshippers of an ancient Sun God. I sit down. As the sun caresses my skin, the fragrance of warm oak wood enters my nostrils.

Like many Christian churches, La Seu, the Roman catholic cathedral in Catalan-gothic style, was built on the site of a pre-existing mosque. Lying above the old Roman citadel, it overlooks the emerald and turquoise Mediterranean and you sometimes still hear the late afternoon Asr prayers calling to the island from the southern coasts, while a breeze wafts along the mouth-watering smell of spiced couscous with roasted almonds.

Visiting this Tierra Sagrada*, I am moored to the full spectrum of bright colours falling down from the rosette shaped windows. In this house I am linked to the beauty of Nature. Is this world not meant to be one wonderful big House, in which we can make love, create compassion and culture? As well as separation, skirmish and suffering, if we choose so… I ponder over it while the light enters me. It makes me think in the colours of my heart.

February 2014

* Holy Earth

At the Camino de Santiago de Compostela, 2014

El Camino de Santiago de Compostela

During the last weeks of July of the summer of 2014, I visited Santiago de Compostela for its university. My Spanish studies this year included one residential week at this prestigious university, which, with over five centuries of history, is known to be one of the best in Spain. I imagine it attracted philosophers, searchers and thinkers amongst the peregrinos, the pilgrims on their Camino. Santiago became a 'highway of knowledge', a diffuser of the great cultural and artistic movements that emerged in Europe some centuries ago.

Imagine, until the ninth century, this town was all forest, named Libredón. In its middle was a Roman Sepulchre and there, in the ruins of its primitive burial grounds, it is said the remains of one of Jesus' apostles, Santiago, were discovered. The majestic Santiago de Compostela Cathedral was built on top of it, and the town became one of Europe's most popular places of Christian pilgrimage.

Not for Christian reasons, but for my own personal and spiritual quest, I walked my one-day stage of the Camino. From Santiago de Compostela through the old oak groves towards Finis terrae 'the end of the world', on the Fisterra-Muxía Way. The weather was hot, the landscape mountainous and my untrained body struggled with diarrhoea.

But it was great! It was quiet on the Camino with 22 whole kilometres to contemplate. Then, when I thought I was lost, I met a wonderful woman and helper, as happens on the Camino.

During the sleepless night afterwards I was reminded of another Spanish route I had taken some years ago. With the sweet memories of the relationship that followed, the 'poem' below came into being. Just before my travel I read about Cheryl Strayed's thousand miles' hike, and I agree with her when she writes in her book Wild, "There's no way to know what makes one thing happen and not another. What leads to what. What causes what to flourish or take another course…"

I still see her
walking towards me
in the old olive grove
Ripe and juicy like the new green harvest and
mysterious as the wild trees themselves in their
being, coming from another realm
It was somewhere down south

I saw her again
This time she came from the north
walking towards Fisterra (fini-tierra) like I did
A peregrina
Each step of her 800 kilometres carried by her maternal guru
we shared a part of the camino
sparkles on the path of our lives
reaching these green valleys of paradise
'¡Buena suerte con tu vida!'*

July 2014

* Lots of luck in your life!

Street Palma, 2011

The shutters

Doors and windows. There is a folder full of them in my photo-archive. They can be so symbolic, can't they? Openings into another realm or a different reality… We speak of 'windows of opportunity' and here at Findhorn we work a lot with Eileen Caddy's 'Opening Doors Within' guidance. On the material level, the door is the entrance and exit, the passage into a building. Sometimes the windows look like the eyes of the house.

Several summers ago, during a journey through the south of France, I worked with the theme of windows and doors; their colours, potential and deeper meaning. They became the focus of that photo-travel. Les portes et les fenêtres. Les yeux ouvertes ou fermés, qui me regardent, qui me parlent – et moi, j'ecoute. Et on se regarde, nous deux. *

In one quick movement, this window, with its turquoise closed shutters in the bright afternoon sunshine, called my attention. Was the Madame of the house having a well-deserved siesta? I imagine a late fulfilling lunch with friends, with Poisson aux legumes, freshly baked baguette and a bottle of Sauvignon de l'Arjolle, a crisp white wine from their Languedoc region?

Was hers the happy story I pictured? Or do we make our stories reflecting our own mood? Are they filled with our dreams and longings like shutters opening and closing to expose the film of our life?

These windows have their eyes closed to the world, looking inwards, and I cannot read life in between the hinged wooden panels. But in the shade of the lush green tree my eyes keep moving upwards wanting the story to continue.

January 2014

* *Doors and windows, eyes open or closed, which look at me, which speak to me – and I, I listen. And we look at each other.*

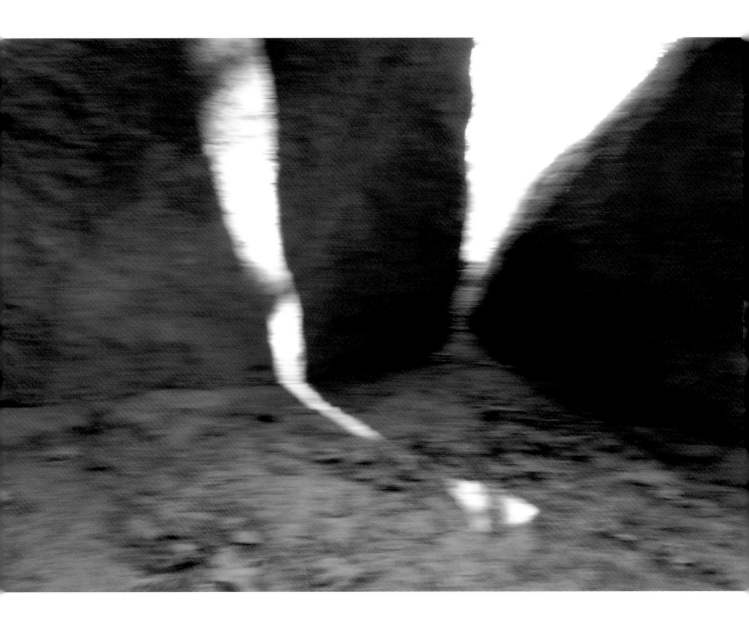

Hunnebed Zeegse, Netherlands, 2011

A Crack in Time

For seven years I lived in the north-east of the Netherlands, in the provinces of Groningen and Drenthe, where all the 54 still existing Dutch 'hunebedden' can be found. I revisited some this spring. A 'hunebed' or dolmen is a kind of cairn or cromlech. They were built as part of a northern megalithic culture some 5,500 years ago. It is said these dolmen, once covered with earth, were burial chambers. Maybe I'll still find a potshard or a bead.

The mysterious collection of boulders plays its own timeless role. 'There's a crack in everything, that's where the light comes in...'* The light arrives from thousands of years back between these huge hunebed stones. I crawl inside, under the covering stones and, lying on the soft, slightly damp earth, I connect with the powerful energies of the place. And for a little while, which could be an eternity, I breathe with the ones buried deep under here. Sometimes I come with a question, sometimes I come with a gift; but always I leave enriched.

Zeegse/Tynaarlo, Drente, the Netherlands 2011

* Leonard Cohen

Spring in Scotland

"Seize the moment," my Spanish friend, Maria Jesus, says. "It's an expression in English," she explains. It is what I seem to be doing, she can tell from my face.

I have come inside our office with an ice cream, a Solero Exotic. If I am eating ice cream, then please let it be a Solero Exotic. It reminds me of my friend Greet in the Netherlands, who, for many summers, was an ice cream seller. Through the streets she would ring her bell, or go to the public parks and playing grounds; places where people go to feel a holiday feeling.

That is how I feel, that is what is on my face, blossoming a little with the first suntan from an early February sun. So bright, so sunny, so warm. I had forgotten the sun's existence. Imagine it will be spring again! It will be summer again! We will go outside. We will hang out at the beach, or on the terraces with cool drinks, without all those layers of clothes on. Our bags will be filled with sun protector factor 10. Suddenly the whiteness of our skin will pigment itself into a healthy warm brown tint. Suddenly the trees will lose their transparency and green will be nature's favourite fashion colour again. Imagine! Gone, the long shadows and the early dusks. No more arriving at work in the dark before dawn. Soon, no more leavings at 5 pms like midnight, trying to find our way home night-blinded on the pitch-dark unlit paths of The Park in Findhorn.

Done with it! Over. There won't be just moon and stars; there will be sun, visible.

The morning will awake before milking time, before Graham delivers his fish from his van, and before the first cars leave the parking lot of my home at Culbin Sands Apartments. Along with the birds, the trees, and the bees, I am looking forward to this exotic wonderful possibility, which seems to be entirely outside reality most of the time here in the north. Just wait and keep on imagining… It's really going to be spring in Scotland again!

12 February 2008

White tree blossoms, Forres, 2015

A pilgrimage walk at Skye

I went to the Isle of Skye for some days and once again the immense beauty of Scottish nature overwhelmed me. The lochs. The seas. The moors. The ancient mountains rocking. Streams and waterfalls replenishing me through ears and skin. Rusty ferns on gentle hills holding us.

I walked my own little pilgrimage walk near Shiel Bridge on an old single track through a rusty fern valley flowing with the coastline. As the colours intensified I stepped on the earth, following earlier footsteps, from one village or settlement to another in this long valley. I had to cross a noisy stream and slowed my feet until I walked with the earth and with the stream. And they were with me, those thousands of women who had walked here before me, alone by foot, or with an animal or cart to transport their goods to trade or to visit their blood family. I followed their feet.

The sky with its remarkable roof of autumnal leaves became my cairn. The air I breathed was sacred air. I walked and met the many wonderful faces of God and I smiled back, while my heart filled itself with light and tender joy and I became as large as the hills and the valley; I became the landscape and all that was, all that is.

Gratitude for eyes to see; for a heart to open. Thank You!

6 June 2011

Landscape Glenelg, Isle of Skye, 2008

The cows at Loch Fada

The Isle of Skye is a fascinating island on the Scottish west coast. From Findhorn it is quite a journey, but even the travel towards is a worthwhile experience. Meandering along Loch Ness (Nessy appeared to me once, on a very dark winter's day). Driving through the Highlands. Meeting the mountains, moors and many lochs. A bridge connects the mainland at Kyle of Lochalsh with the island itself. I love trekking between the peat-coloured hills. There are deserted farmhouses. In the middle of nowhere cattle crossing the road, gates open. The fresh water of the long lake 'Loch Fada' in the near distance. Cows and young bulls, reminding me of home and the farm in the polder I grew up in. When the young cows come outside for the first time, they don't know yet how to use all their four feet and they jump all over the place. Almost as if they are trying to fly.

15 December 2011

Cows at Loch Fada, Isle of Skye, 2008

Loving Iona

Today I saw the fine detailed images of nature spirits,
drawn by Findhorn artist Francis Ripley:
Spirits of the Wind on Iona.
Three flashes, bird faces with a direction
to go in, energy moving at the speed of sound.
I recognized them.

I have felt their velvet touch. On mild May days
they give us green young meadows … bleating with lambs…

I have felt their November storms, their tough blows
blinding the mind, the view and
sweeping me into the waves. The water,
that has brought so many strangers to this ancient island.
Coming home.

Columba with the western wind, the Vikings with the
northern winds – the blood of the monks renaming the white beach
Traigh Bhan nam Manach
and all women who fled the eilan –
the sounds of sorrow.
Spirit of the wind carry me.

17 March 2006

White beach of the monks, Iona, 2014

Time & Place

Time is an odd phenomenon don't you think? I'll give you an example, but you'll have your own. Last week I went to the isle of Iona on the Scottish west coast. Cannot remember how long it is since I was last there, surely years! How could it be, that on arriving, I felt as if I had only left it the previous month, or even week? Everything felt so familiar: its sea of the 'Sound of Iona', its colourful rocks, its Traigh Bhan nam Manach, (the White Beach of the Monks); with the house Traigh Bhan and Robbie, the warm Rayburn, inviting us to bake our own bread and spend lots of time in its cosy kitchen… On Iona time runs differently.

Time slips, time loss or a déjà vu, all happen much more easily during these days at the end of October and the beginning of November; around Hallowe'en or Samhain, the Celtic festival of New Year in the Wheel of the Year, in the Wheel of Time. It is said that this is when the veil between the dimensions is thinner, making it easier to connect to the invisible world, the 'other side'. This practice happened In many cultures: by the Native Americans, by the Celtic druids; even the Christians copied it from the Celts and called it All Saints Day and All Souls Day. Time to honour the beloved ones who no longer inhabit human bodies.

In our physical world a lot of us believe in the separation: 'here' are the living, 'there' are the dead. But maybe we all are living souls and we are not as separated as we think? Maybe there are more dimensional shifts. I like to believe that. My birthday is during in this Samhain time, and I'm interested in this 'twilight zone' in which time and sometimes even spaces overlap. Time only seems to exist for observers inside our universe. It is said that even physicists, although having trouble with this 'problem of time' or conundrum, cannot ignore it. Who would want to? It's fascinating!

This is a favourite photo I took of the colourful rocks at the north side of Iona. There is a deep pool or hole inside, maybe to disappear and swim to the 'other side'?

November 2014

Red rocks at the northern beaches of Iona, 2007

Burn the clavie

BURN THE CLAVIE!
BURN THE CLAVIE!
old barrel wood and oil and tar
blackness
on fire!
shouting primal chanting men
and we answering
our screams
HOYA! FIRE !
flames
hissing spitting gripping tearing
BURN THE CLAVIE!
swept by the crowd pushed carried
away by the flames
the red fire that
called the pagan woman in me
yelling hissing spitting.
A fire being
more tar more oil more
red and orange
then black clouds filling
our skies our earth.
We burn the clavie!
Coal smears in our hair
our bodies still filled
with fire
as we see the ghost leave
and the sky lifts
and later we go home to our clan
with a half burned wood barrel
which will bring us luck
for a full year.
Happy new year!

Burghead, 11th January 2011

Clavie ritual Burghead, 2004

Hopeman's Cove

These rocks are part of Hopeman's Cove Bay, on the north-east coast of Scotland. Imagine these rocks once being part of a hot desert, where the Sahara is now. Its sand dunes still are preserved in the colourful rocks. Two totally different rock formations, or world citizens, banged into each other and unified forever. Tracing the hot winds in the white sandrock with my lingering fingers while my feet try to keep sturdy, standing on the battered chilly northern coast… Since the Ice Age, the whispers of the burning desert have always won over the battle cries of the north, and they still fill my heart with longing and belonging…

November 2012

Hopeman's cove, 2009

Being independent or being inter-dependent?

It might be that this coming month Scotland, 'my' country – as I live here – gains independence from the United Kingdom. And maybe not. With joy I received my poll card for The Scottish Independence Referendum.

It feels as such an honour to vote for this on 18 September: the choice of independence for a country, without any war needing to be fought first. Having the choice of voting Yes or voting No. The Referendum brings up lots of discussion, including in our Findhorn Foundation Community and I think this to be very positive, whatever the outcome will be. A neighbour's window, which declares: "Hope not fear, Dare to vote Yes", makes me smile every time I pass it.

I just learned that it is not Scotland's first attempt to be independent; the oldest surviving document about this fact is from 1320 when the Scots issued a 'declaration of independence' to be freed from English aggression and its dominating power and become its own sovereignty. Not far away from Findhorn lies Culloden Battlefield, an old wound in the country's history.

But personally I feel this independence moves away from the past and has all to do with the people wishing to decide their own future, more than Hollyrood (where the Scottish government resides) can do now.

This all reminds me of my own and our inter-dependence. I live alone and although I am not depending on a special relationship and as such could be called 'an independent woman' in the traditional sense, in the modern sense I am as inter-dependent as anybody else, as a human being. We all are depending, in the first place on nature, on the Earth. But we also depend on our friends, in a light – hopefully healthy – way, as they depend on us. I am inter-dependent on my customers, friends and acquaintances, people who already know my graphic and photo work, who for instance ask me to do some design work for their business or who buy some notebooks from my studio or a photo book from the online web shop… We serve each other.

So, if it is a Yes, may we become neighbours who serve each other well, who realise we are inter-dependent, as well as part of Europe.

August 2014

Your
polling
Centre
...e

JAMES MILNE INSTITUTE
43 FINDHORN
FORRES
IV36 3YF

Polling Station No 82

...mber - MM0801/92

Scottish Indep
OFFICIA
The Mor.

A M BIJMAN
N SANDS
NTS

This card is for informati
without it, but it will save
polling station and show
Check if your polling pl

"How far is't called to Forres?"

"How far is't called to Forres?" was Shakespeare's Macbeth's famous question to the three Weird Sisters, or witches. Later, like many, the women probably were tried for witchcraft in Cluny Hills Hollow or burned at the stake. Macbeth is now the name of the local prize-winning game and venison butcher.

Seen from The Park, the nearest town, Forres, always looked quite far away to me, emotionally at least. But actually, now that I have moved to Forres, and commute everyday by bike or bus between my studio in the Park and my new home, I realise this is not true. Forres is home to Cluny Hill, to Newbold, to Transition Town and other familiar Findhorn Foundation Community organisations, businesses and people I know.

Spring, while the soil puts forth new beginnings, is a good time to move house. Blossoms smile along the streets, and in the many parks that enrich this little town and now enrich me. At Castehill Park, I feel feasted under the arch of pastel pink, ivory white and rose red Japanese cherry trees. Forres has more green to discover in depth. Grant Park, Sanquhar Woodlands, Bogton Park, Rose Garden, and Cluny Hills, with its winding paths around the four or five hills filled with woods of Scots pine and larch.

Despite its surroundings being clothed with trees since early times, probably the name Forres neither derives from forest, as I always thought, nor from the gaelic Far-uís (near the water) but is a heritage from the time of the Roman Invasion. (My goodness, did they come this far north? What were they looking for in this rough climate and remote land, when they could indulge in sunny palaces with Roman baths with bronzed gladiators who were queuing up to massage them?) Anyway, one of those Romans marked this place on the map as Varis, from which Forres derived. As said, probably. Earlier it was also probably, the Picts who erected the esteemed but mysterious Sueno's Stone, which still stands as guardian to the north entrance of the town. More than 500 years ago, Forres was granted a charter by the king to become a Royal Burgh, although another king, oops, was murdered in its castle. Once the whole town of wooden buildings was completely destroyed by fire, once half flooded. Alongside all this drama, there also is the glorious history of once being a chief town in Moray. I like to fantasize about all that happened here in the past, but I did not invent most of this information. I found it in a delicate little book, written in 1894. The local library let me take it home to read. We'll never know what was really true and what not…

After living a decade at the seaside, with carpets of yellow gorse, broom and purple heather, with the sounds of yelling seagulls, I notice the differences in my new residence. So many other bird songs, a dawn chorus! Such different vegetation, and even different water. The Mosset Burn meanders through town before joining 'our' river Findhorn towards Findhorn Bay; there we are on familiar ground. As new I walk through streets with ancient buildings on soil that remembers the passions of the past.

It is not very far, that's for sure. Aye!

May 2015

Castehill, Forres, 2015

Lossiemouth's delights

Despite my illness, I am working on a book, as if a deeper creativity still wants to express itself. The work has progressed from five different addresses I stayed at this year. I am hoping to hang on longer, as well as finish the book, in my next accommodation, at Pine Court in Forres. I feel like a nomad. Since mid-July this year I have even become officially labelled as 'disabled homeless', living for six weeks in a homeless-care flat, provided by Moray Council in Bishopmill, a dull grey looking outskirt of Elgin. Too far from what I call home, too far from my community.

But what is good is that the flat lies on the number 33 bus route from Elgin to Lossiemouth. I had not visited this picturesque village, called The Jewel of the Moray Firth, for at least five years. Originally the port belonging to Elgin, it became a significant fishing town. But this is history now, like for most harbours at the Moray Firth. Its economy has been very dependent on the RAF base at Lossiemouth. With its now 6,800 inhabitants it is growing in popularity. I am not interested though in the residential areas, with their many RAF and holiday houses. I come for the sea! I come for the river Lossie! I come for the unique land and seascape, with its wide open skies and the flocks of birds.

The village has a lengthy boulevard along the beach and the incoming river Lossie. A long row of colourful triangle flags charmingly decorates the promenade, making it look even more like the friendly coastal holiday village it is. The river Lossie arrives meandering under a wobbly footbridge, curving itself into the open sea. This leaves a generous end area of dunes between the two waters, giving the many day-visitors the choice of a sunny or a shady side to spend time in. It is a lovely place for families, and, on sunny summer days, the beaches are showered with sand castles, flashy beach towels and shouting lads and lassies. During my LCG time (Living in Community Guest programme of the Findhorn Foundation) we visited 'Lossie' for one long afternoon group bonding time. And that same first summer in Findhorn, in 1998, I stayed a weekend in a B&B on its hill, with splendid sea views. I simply fell in love. Lossie has kept a special place in my heart since then, although I did not drop by on a regular basis.

Now, in 2016, things have changed and during these six weeks it is a joy to see Lossiemouth so frequently. The number 33 bus drops us off at the boulevard itself, close to the best ice cream parlour in Moray: Miele's of Lossie. There, an Italian family makes, or one could say creates, yummy homemade ice cream, displaying it in the abundant and fashionable Mediterranean way, like I have seen Madrileños and the natives of Palma and Malaga do. At Miele's, even their choice of gluten-free ice cream is remarkable. During these weeks living in Elgin, I indulge myself with regular visits to the sea and the ice cream shop. Lossie is well known for its ice cream, as only two doors along from Miele's is its competitor, Rizza. Many like myself have made their choice: never have I seen queues waiting outside Rizza.

I take dangerous risks, crossing the busy road walking on only one crutch, holding the other one under my left arm, while this hand tries to keep the two gigantic scoops of luxurious ice cream in the cone and not smear the road and pavement with it. Until I reach the other side, grass, a bench to fall down onto, can I fully enjoy the view and my saved ice cream. Sigh! Every time, both are splendid. Just delicious.

Elgin, 24 August 2016

Beach-flowers,
2010

Listen

Pine Court, the pines long gone, but birds find new trees

Listen.
Even the wind is searching the silence in the street
Between the ongoing vibrations on the asphalt,
The buses, six per hour, the 31, the 11 and the 10, always too late,
The lorries loaded with tree trunks and
The cars in haste, speeding like a crime is chasing them.
Pedestrians thudding the pavement, the sporty shoes of the students
Dressed as a flock of crows,
The ticking of the elders with one walking stick only,
Women heavy with shopping bags, the lunch-, tea- or dinner-pot waiting.
An ongoing show of humanity on a stage.
My stage.
Trees breathing out.
Beyond all the sun does not mind, just loves to be
In charge of the lightning.
Listen.
The grass, the shrubs remember the dark.
Noise failing.
While the chairs and garden table on the balcony look out for the butterflies in the lilac buddleia in the corner, the promise of
fragrance of the dark red peonies, the blue wild cornflowers, the orange crocosmia, the red balls on the pelargonium next to
the sliding doors. Here or there. In or out.
All night long the street is asleep. All night long the birds, awake, make their own song. Trees breathing in.
And I sigh in my sleep and hear the whispers of the arriving autumn air, soon waking up in their warm colours. My favourites.
Listen.

Forres, 12 September 2016

Tree blossoms, Forres, 2016

I believe in angels

My attention was drawn to some lines of a Spanish poem (1) ; in my translation it says: "Roots and wings. That the wings may take root and the roots may fly."

The first music I danced to, on my visit to an Experience Week at Findhorn more than 20 years ago, was the song 'I believe in angels' and from that moment on, I actually did. Or rather I started to believe, but it was about believing in a different kind of angel to the Roman Catholic guardian angels I had grown up with; now I opened up to the idea of intelligent beings existing in nature - the kind that Dorothy MacLean (2) calls 'Devas'. They are close to the flora, the fauna, landscapes, cities and even to us, people. They are not like faeries or other existing 'little people' in the natural realm.

This was all new to me then, but it made so much sense! I can now see angels as part of the metaphysical realm, being present in the air and of vital, integral importance to all life. It helps me to know that there are higher beings or universal forces out there, beings that see me, love me, know me and give support, inspiration and encouragement. We are not alone! I repeat this every morning and thank them. It makes a difference and I can recommend it to you.

Dorothy says that every place has its own 'Landscape' Angel. So I imagine Findhorn beach has one too. And on a beautiful day during a walk along the beach of sand and pebbles at Moray Firth, I suddenly looked up into the bright blue sky. There I saw this shape or figure appear, in between the clouds; like a heart, like an angel… Do you see it in the photo?

Here at Findhorn we knew Frances Ripley as a remarkable woman and community member. She made many subtle drawings of the Nature Spirits. In her book 'Visions Unseen' she writes how "they have the capacity to show themselves in a variety of forms, or else as formless swirls of colour and light". Wow. Well, yes … that's what I saw…! So I sat a bit more on that beach enjoying 'my' angel. Until the wind took her away…

It is all in the air, all around us, to give us life – with every breath. The Breath of Life.

February 2015

(1) 'Raices y alas."Pero que las alas arraiguen y las raíces vuelen." by Spanish poet Juan Ramón Jiménez, 'Diario de un poeta recién casado', Madrid 1916

(2) Dorothy MacLean, Co-founder of the Findhorn Foundation Community https://www.findhorn.org/aboutus/vision/history/ #.VOT3FFozjfg

(3) Frances Ripley 'Visions Unseen' , read more in Brian Nobbs' review: http://www.findhorn.org/2008/09/visions-unseen-by-frances-ripley/#.VOT7s1ozjfg

Sky above Findhorn beach, 2004

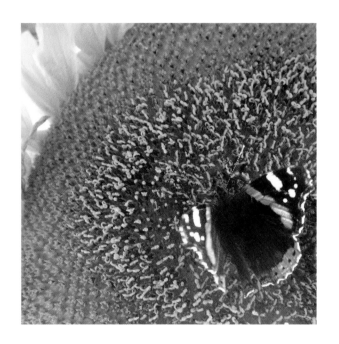

Fervent gardener 1 - Cullerne Garden

I've always been a fervent gardener. I worked in Findhorn Foundation's Cullerne Garden for eight years, some of it as a staff member. I took the flower area under my wing and loved the responsibility and freedom to make it blossom. With a Foundation Year Programme (FYP) student I created Flowershare for subscribers from May until October. Each week we gave them each a bucket brimming with flowers. From spring flowers like tulips, aquilegias and pasqueflowers, then peonies, anthemis, marguerites and calendulas in midsummer, until the autumn colours of dahlias, chrysanthemum and a multitude of drying flowers. We grew 300 dahlias in many varieties, dozens of which I had bought directly from the growers in the bulb area of Hillegom in the Netherlands, near where I had lived. The flower area expanded and we sold many creative bunches in the Phoenix shop three times a week. They brightened the caravans in the Findhorn Bay Caravan Park, the Community Centre, as well as some Foundation offices and departments. Sometimes in midsummer, when on early morning Sunday tunnel duty, I would pick more flowers, make them into beautiful bunches between my official duties of watering the veggies in the polytunnels, fields and cold frames. Then I'd take them down to the Community Centre and sell them to everyone having brunch. After I left the garden, the flowers area and production decreased and sales hardly happen anymore; there are other priorities now.

I am aware I'm more or less blowing my own trumpet here. It is because I did a good job gardening. But most likely I was not such a nice person to work with.

I loved gardening and worked very hard. During all the Foundation programmes I attended, I attuned to serve in Cullerne Garden as my Living Education Department. For eight years from spring 1998, Cullerne was my school of life. I learned some tough lessons there, but Cullerne also helped me soften my blunt Dutch countryside way of communicating. Looking back, working and growing in these gardens has been a fabulous experience, for which I am very grateful.

Findhorn, 1 May 2016

Being young and visible, my 'Youth @ Findhorn' project

Youth. Young people. Gosh, it's easy to forget we've all been young ourselves. Every generation seems to express this period in its own, new way. Before last year, seeing youngsters at the bus stop, hidden under their hoods, sometimes made me feel uncomfortable. Then I remembered my own teenage years, which were the worst of my life. I was living in the countryside, going to school in a small village. I was so unhappy, insecure and damaged. I tried to hide it by acting the opposite way. I remember a photo of me when I was 15, and now I feel a lot of compassion for the girl I was then. Without judgement or rejection. When you have children, you often relive these years during their adolescence, but I don't have nor do I live with young people myself here.

This all made me want to get to know more about the young people of nowadays. The youth around me live in a rural area like I do. I felt curious (and courageous at times) to photograph and interview them for a project I called Youth @ Findhorn.

Many people in Findhorn know my photographic work of landscapes, flowers, seascapes; they know my community event photos and books. "Why suddenly people?" they ask. In the past I photographed – in waves – non-human nature and people. Activists, female farmers, 50+ women, habitants of a rural village. Some of these projects have become books. Working with people can be intense, satisfying and demanding, I tell you; a flower does not comment or resist being portrayed. Humans or nature; in either situation I have to connect from my heart with them to get the best results.

I contacted the young people and interviewed them about their homelife, education or work; their hopes and aspirations for their future; what living in a village, especially Findhorn, is like. I had to have their parents' written agreement. The families read back the interview, and we made corrections together. They helped choose the photographs I used and they saw the edited summary of the text. In most cases this was a graceful process. Some people did not want to be part of the project and some others withdrew during, alas.

Looking back I think the young people shown in the series were very brave. The series shows their hopes, sometimes their insecurity, but often their strength and wisdom. It felt like an honour to make them visible and to help other people to get to know this group better. As some visitors at the exhibition at the Moray Art Centre wrote as feedback: "Extraordinary & deeply inspiring work. Mesmerising," or, "Thank you for giving a very interesting insight into this unusual and privileged group of children."

That is indeed what I wanted: to allow these wonderful young people to be seen and heard.

October 2014

Young people from Findhorn, 2013/2014

Ceilidh dancing in the Universal Hall, Findhorn, 2011

Moving, dancing, swirling around

This picture is a favourite dance image. Look at those odd movements made during Scottish Ceilidh dances! What are they all about?

We're fortunate to have lots of dance performances, shows and workshops here at Findhorn. Since the start of our community, creative expression has been important. In 1975 Bernard Wosien brought the sacred circle dances to Findhorn. Here they received a home, developed and later on circled outwards, using the Findhorn way of attunement, sharing and blessing, into the rest of the world. In the 90s the Celtic Festivals with Peter Vallance brought new kinds of dances. Nowadays there are a huge variety of dance practices, from Biodanza and 5 Rhythms to Astroshamanic Trance Dance.

It's all about moving, dancing, swirling around and around… And this is how my life feels at the moment. Spring has arrived, securing new beginnings. But where did the idea that those beginnings would only bring positive change spring from? Every tiny fragile new tree bud knows it will magically blossom in the spring sunshine, accompanied by a gentle rain now and then. But while opening into a delicate blossom it might be surprised by a spring shower or even by an all-destructive wind and hail storm. It's taking a huge risk in showing itself. It will be moved, danced and swirled around and its strength will be severely tested. It must be in for a bit of a blow.

And so must we! Like the blossoms, our own new beginnings are not guaranteed to start positively. You don't need to tell me about that one, as I am, shifted, switched and swirled around by life. Some roughly opened old scars about love and trust reveal 'the mess I made' (free to Amy Winehouse's song): loss, disappointment and grief under the anger. It can be a long lasting dance into the exhaustion of resist. Or until a fresh wind brings the insight that actually a good thing is happening: old perceptions need to be challenged and pains released first, gently or by force. Does this all come from a deeper need to heal and grow? Is that its main reason for materializing in our lives? As long as I engage with, submit and surrender myself to the movements of this dance, while seeing it as a kind of spring clean before I myself can spring into the new beginnings of my own inner springtide, I know somehow it will be fine. I will be fine.

So, let's dance, "let's dance the feelings, the tears and the passion".* Come on, I found some beautiful blossoms for your hair.

29 March 2014

*from a poem by Marieta Maglas, 2010 (http://www.poemhunter.com/marieta-maglas/poems/)

Home is here

In the morning, I witness the demolishing of the caravan next door, 203 Pineridge or Anna's, as older community members called the mobile home. Once, years ago, it was a good home to me, as well as to many others. So, I say, "Thank you caravan." Lately Park Maintenance used it as storage. Now it is gone, my 'garden' becomes larger. Further away are the new neighbours. The bay tree already looks different on its own, and I guess the eucalyptus enjoys the wider view as much as I will, when the rubbish is cleared.

The same morning, I discover another new neighbour, just around the corner. The land located as 213 Pineridge now hosts a friendly round yurt. I witness Lois swinging with joy in and around it, and I recognise her joy. After eight years of caravans and eco-houses, I know that the level of happiness and home feeling is not defined by outer appearances. Do we not often hang on more to our old but cosy armchair or half broken shed, with its history, than to a new one?

Back at Pineridge, and my sweet home the caravan Chez Albert, where I have lived only since the winter. You might see here the ridge landscape of a desolated holiday park at the end of the season, waiting for planning permission. You might see here a ridge of unhealthily bare pine trees. That might all be true. But my heart sees a little happy palace on a green estate, through which the sun rises and sets, and rises again. Where I could stay and live happily ever after (if we can have broadband please). A dilemma, as I have been told to move out of here by the end of June, so theoretically I had better start looking for something else. But I cannot yet, too early for the honeymoon-heart.

An idea I can imagine though is that a particular place is preparing itself to call me home. It is in The Park or in Findhorn village I think. Heaven knows which things still need to change place, move along, switch side, pack and go –

May it all be blessed.
May It Be.
And then, I will come.
Just let me know.

Spring 2006

Changing home and house hunting is quite a regular thing in the Findhorn Foundation Community where there is, like in Findhorn village, a lack of accommodation. I myself have regularly gone through the process. In 2006, leaving my staff job at the Findhorn Foundation, I had to find my own accommodation in the area. I went for the summer to Forres and then in September, I found flat 3 and later flat 28 at Culbin Sands Apartments at the sea in Findhorn village, where I lived until in March 2015.

Lobelia plant on table in garden; Chez Albert caravan

View from 28 Culbin Sands Apartments, Findhorn, June 2013

A view

I moved house this week, to a wonderful apartment with a fabulous view. Culbin Sands Apartments at Findhorn still carries in its attics and cellars the pain of its past as the Culbin Sands Hotel, which was said to be haunted, and much earlier, when the Viking warriors stepped onto the land here and soaked the soil with blood. So much healing is needed, as well as joyful energy. I'm doing my best. Let me tell you:

This apartment, rejuvenated, wants to be celebrated

While the smell of paint and varnish has hardly vanished

While many boxes full of life and release still wait to be opened and integrated

The walls still bare

Before my images fingerprint them.

But the summer solstice sun and the full moon call for it now

While the blooming gorse reflects on the walls

While endless skies and seas invite themselves in, to be discovered by experienced eyes still

so curious.

So I give thanks to all involved

And let us bless this place with Joy and Healing

To be my new Home.

Summer Solstice 20 June 2013

My home until spring 2015

Fervent gardener 2

My love for gardening started long before I worked in Cullerne Gardens, where I mostly cared for the flowers. As a young girl living on a farm in one of the Dutch polders, I helped my father in the garden, which provided us with vegetables all year round. We ate them freshly picked in the summer, when we children were also helping to fill preserving jars with pickled partly-cooked fruits and vegetables like French beans, cauliflower and sweet peas. They lined the cellar shelves, ready for the winter months. My father let me choose the flower seeds from the catalogues. I always loved dahlias, as did he, and we tried out many different varieties. Lupins though were not allowed in our garden. I think it was because my mother had loved them a lot and they reminded him too much of her after her death.

Later on, living in the north of the country, I created a big garden myself. After a year of growing vegetables, I started to concentrate on fruit growing: strawberries in rows, next to apple and pear trees, cherries and berries. Vegetables were given to me in abundance by the neighbouring women, who had them in plenty in their gardens. Nobody grew fruit, and I am very fond of it.

In Forres, where I lived last year, I turned two weed plots – the front and back garden – into my little paradise: flowers and bushes at the front, vegetables, herbs and strawberries at the back of the house. Such a joy!

Now it is May again, and although snow was forecast for this coming weekend, the sun is out. The chalet, my temporary home in The Park, has a south-facing terrace and herb bed, both yelling to be tended. The gardener in me can't wait to respond. Weeding is the first thing that needs to be done. With the physical condition I have at the moment – which includes vertigo, constant dizziness and distorted eyesight – it seems an overwhelming and Herculean task. I do not know how to begin gardening again. Kneeling to do the job? No! Squatting? No way. OK … sitting and moving on the ground then? That might work… Oh my goodness! Is this something all less able people have to go through? I never knew.

I am painfully clumsy, like a drunken sailor. For an hour and a half I try to 'keep calm and keep weeding', puffing and sighing as the world swirls around with every move of my head, until I have to give up and give in to the nausea. It is the most disappointing and frustrating experience I have had in this last half year here in The Park.

But OK, I pruned the sage. I weeded three metres of terrace tiles. I tackled a big, long-rooted nettle family. They'll end up in tonight's soup. With quite some effort I did fill more than half a brown compost wheelie bin with weeds and old branches. I did it! I am proud to have gardened again.

Findhorn, 1 May 2016

The smell of salt

Not far from my house the sea, and the endless beach
With its pebbles, perform an ever changing seascape.
There is my home.

The smell of salt, the taste of water, the touch of cold waves
around the feet, creeping up the calves, changing the body into
a vessel of goose bumps.
Standing, looking over –

I play with the pebbles at the beach to be a child again.
To forget time. To be, only here, only now.
I feel the roughened softness of the sand sticking on the wet pebbles.
Their shape in my hands. Their colours in my eyes.
Their smell of horizons, their memory of long-forgotten shores
Entering my heart
While I surrender to this sweet invasion.

What is it really about? You ask. It is about the beach and me.
How we belong together.
That I feel touched while I touch the soft sand
The undulations of her skin and I see I am built like Her, in Her image.
I am water. I am soft, rough, uneven, broken though delicate.
This beach is calling me again and again.
I am Hers. In all weather.

And you ask me why I so often go to the beach, why I always long
for the water. My whole life I have been living close to the water.
The lake with its reed mace waterfront touching the polder land.
The canals in the towns. Expecting the ships to come home with damask
brought back from distant shores.

January 2009

Findhorn Beach , World Beach Project (pebble tower 8), 2009

New and ancient love at Findhorn Bay

Wide. Spacious. Too much almost. Skies without a ceiling to breathe in. Miles of sandy soil to be on, to walk on. Step by step. My footsteps are new here, stranded from another shore at the other side of the North Sea. And every step opens the curtain of a theatre. Come with me, get closer and see in close-up the lichen on the old heather branches. Open in winter, covered by the Erica flowers in spring and autumn. Come in early summer and you will be overwhelmed by a carpet of yellow with the smell of coconut. The gorse often blossoms a second time in winter and shows it is snow proof.

I live at the end of Findhorn village near the dunes and its sea, on the crossing of the Findhorn Bay, where the river of the same name comes meandering in and meets the Moray Firth. The beach is different here. Every day. The shoreline changes continuously throughout the day.

The beach can be a small stroke of large pebbles at high tide. It can be a desert of sand far into what before was sea; far behind the Findhorn banks, where the seals bathe in the sunshine. Close to the place where once was land. Where the old village sank down centuries ago. From where they found the urn with the old women's ashes. Her heart full of ancient love is still buried in the bay while she holds the new village. She still remembers the monks of Kinloss Abbey demanding taxes from the homecoming salmon fishermen. She still remembers the women on the pier at the harbour looking out for their men. And of course she remembers the young boys longing to be sailors.

Come sit with me on the sand and taste the marram grass. Listen with her to the hypnotising sound of the waves coming home. Lay down. See that sky above the church? We'll have rain soon. Or it will blow over to Nairn.

Let it go. Just stay here with us for a bit.

Findhorn, 9 February 2008

Findhorn Bay, 2012

Living and longing – at the waterfront

Not far from my flat, the sea and the endless sandy beach with its pebbles perform an ever-changing seascape. There is my home. It is the water, a home that will stay, even if I am soon to leave the flat here.

You ask me why I so often go to the beach, why I always long for the water. I have lived my whole life close to the water. The lake at Dorregeest, its reed mace waterfront touching our north-Holland polder land, where my nephew drowned. I remember. The canals of the old Dutch town Haarlem, and the long straight canal between old moorland at Kiel-Windeweer in the north. The Italian harbours, expecting the ships to come home with damask from distant foreign shores. The Adriatic sea, in which one hot summer I myself almost drowned, struggling for life while Cyndi Lauper's 'Girls just wanna have fun' resounded over the entire beach camping.

Nowadays, for almost two decades, my coastline is Scotland's Moray Firth on the northern Atlantic edge of Europe, where the Vikings once fought with the Picts. Our seawater is warmed by the North Atlantic Drift, which we call here the Warm Gulf Stream, maybe just to make it sound warmer. We need that!

I had a free day yesterday, a non-working day. I treated myself to a spa outing with a friend in Nairn, where the air still breathes the traditional seaside resort it was in the 1950s. I loved it! Each in our own way, we enjoyed the water. As steam in the Hamman, as hot bubbles in the Jacuzzi, in the outdoor hot tub, or flowing free in the pool. Even dipping our feet into the still ice-cold sea.

There it was again; the smell of salt, the taste of water, the touch of cold waves around the feet creeping up the calves, changing the body into a vessel of goose bumps. Standing, looking out over the waves. How often do I 'see' the picture of a woman, standing at the waterside, her eyes longing over the horizon to that unknown not lived life, which could have been?

Water is so emotional.

Findhorn, March 2015

Findhorn beach, Beach Project 2009

'Waves are coming in' at Findhorn Beach

I regularly go beachcombing after a high tide, when the pebble beach gives space again to the endless sands. Then I can see the seals sunbathing on the banks far out in the sea where once was a village. Then, especially in spring and autumn, there are lots of 'findings' to catch at this part of the Moray coastline. Plenty of colourful seaweed comes in with the high tides from the deep ocean. Kelp, pod razor shells, red rags, sea oak and lettuce, and all kind of wrack: bladder, flat, horned, knotted or toothed. Sometimes tree stems, branches and leaves in all autumn colours are brought back in by the river water, carrying the memories of a summer in the forests of the Scottish Highlands.

'There is so much magnificence near the ocean

Waves are coming in' *

Findhorn, October 2011

* From So Much Magnificence, as sung by Deva Premal and Mit

Findhorn sea, 2010

Sea Leaves

The sea was offering leaves today. With every wave washed ashore, it threw new leaves at my feet. Spiky pine leaves, autumn brown beech leaves, evergreen ivy leaves. As the waves retreated, they stayed on the sand, held in slowly evaporating foam. Borrowed gifts from the trees along the river becoming sea leaves. They made me stop during my early morning walk at the beach.

From my kitchen window, the sky had looked promising above the little harbour of Findhorn. The northern wind would chase away the grey clouds above the village and I would stay dry on my walk. Coming outside was a bit of a shock. The sun might be springy and up and about earlier each morning, reminding me of long light days, but the wind came from a different direction. Within the three minutes it takes me to reach the beach I was cold through and through, and regretted having brought my fingerless gloves. They are practical for taking photographs, but this morning I had to warm my hands in my pockets after each little series of photos, to prevent me from fainting of the cold. The weather is confused, I thought, this is more autumn, expecting winter to arrive at any moment in floes of ice in the high tide waves.

There was no sand on the beach, only pebbles, and I alternated firmly stepping through them with sauntering my boots through the waterline. Jumping through the threatening tide, playing with the foam, examining the seaweeds, looking for new varieties amongst all the black, brown, greens and greys left on the pebbles. A piece of large wood was brought to my feet the way a cat brings you a mouse. Here, for you. 'Thank you' I said surprised, recognising the bark of a birch. Then there came more. Leaf after leaf washed ashore, being passed from water to shore, carrying memories from the woods along the river Findhorn, stories of releasing, stories of death of loss and of being lost without family, and having to go on. Meandering through the Moray high and lowlands, along meadows and arriving at Findhorn Bay, which flows empty into the warm gulf stream of the Moray Firth. There, rejected by the salt ocean water, the leaves are carried by the seaweeds and thrown ashore some miles from the river mouth, at Findhorn beach. Here in front of my eyes. As a reminder for the day. And I receive the gift, taking with me the scarves and wonders of last autumn.

It will be spring again. With new leaves growing.

Findhorn, March 2008

Seaweed at Findhorn beach, 2008

High Tide Low Tide

Low tide high time
The beach shows me its spread
Its length times its width
Beyond my arms, open wide, stretched
Beyond horizons
It tells me all the time
Look, this is how large you really are.

Findhorn, 29 September 2008

Findhorn beach shoreline, 2008

The sea called me this morning

The sea called me this morning. It had left messages on its creamy sandy shore. Text written in rune language or some coded alphabet unknown to me. Fluent forms. Line shapes. Left with a 3D-pen of vermicelli seaweed. The waves moved the wet shoreline, changing the shades of the mustard coloured sand and slowly changing the messages too.

The sea and the land made a peaceful pact today and allowed the wind to play with them as well as with me. The tide was coming in. Later, lying on the pebbles of the beach I still try to read the messages. I ask the wind to give me some clarity. I touch the earth, opening for a connection with eternity. I look at the waves to infinity.

Findhorn, 16 August 2008

Findhorn Beach Project, 2009

Teasing me

The air was still shaking off another shower
it was a dark night last night
but then
in a myriad of stars, the sky found me
and the wind perfectly
played the echo of their soft giggles
"We got you"
they seemed to sing teasingly
while we all walked home to the ocean.

25 November 2008, on the way home along the Findhorn Bay

Night at Findhorn Bay, 2010

Day and Night, Dark and Light

We're living the longest days of the year here in the northern hemisphere. The nights feel too short to rest from the, at times, overwhelming intensity of the light. Some friends have put up extra curtains to be able to sleep in the dark. A song, well known here in our community, says, "Be still and know that day and night, that dark and light, are one holy circle."

During the last two weeks, three community members left their body to rise into the realm of the Light. Well, after a challenging end in the physical, I believe that's where they'll be going. To the Light.

For this month's entry of my Light Scribble I chose an image of young trees still in blossom in my garden against a dark background, a play of dark and light. The Mother, in one of her guided messages about white flowers tells us in 'The Spiritual Significance of Flowers' that "white light is the light of the Divine Consciousness in its essence. In this white light all other lights are contained and from it they can be manifested, for this reason white also indicates integrality, completeness and totality, especially the integrality of the being in all its parts, from the physical being to the true self."

So take a deep breath. Inhale the light. Let the white flowers enter our heart and let's trust their light will shine on the darkness. To know this brightens my day.

Findhorn, June 2014

Shrub flowers, Culbin Sands Apartments garden, Findhorn, 2013

They shoot the geese

Plop. Plop. They shoot the geese. Does every 'plop' mean one of these wonderful white winged birds tumbles down dead? Broken instinct; a sudden stop to the soaring flight over the Findhorn Bay? One empty space in the V-formation crossing the sky? The one that takes its place, what will she know, what will he feel?

I know so little about the geese or any other big bird. The singing of smaller flying friends sounds through the open window in the early morning. A dawn choir. Their waking-me-up song. Their ode to the new day. Their song of life, now drowned by the sounds of death. So early and already both are present. Plop. Plop. Plop. There is the sound again, now in full spate. Immediately followed up by the songs. Did they hear it too? I carefully pay attention to any differences, any disturbed falling down in tone, any out of harmony sounds…

It does not seem so to me. Or do I simply fail to notice the nuances in their voices, as I neither speak their language nor understand their secret codes?

The Croatian woman in the movie The Secret Life of Words fell silent after the continuous rape, violence and abuse by the occupying groups of soldiers. She fell mute. She told us she would turn off her hearing aid whenever she did not want to hear what was coming.

Plop. Plop.

Findhorn, 11 February 2008

Findhorn Bay, 2009

Schwarzwalderkirschtorte

The sky seems filled with layers tonight
Custard cream and sponge and some deep reds too
like Schwarzwalderkirschtorte
and there, high up, you see that layer
of light?
I will rise
and flow into it
roll myself in it
to be one in heaven's delight

Findhorn, 8 October 2008

Findhorn Bay, 2012

The blessed bramble (1)

My fingertips are deep purple these days. Coloured by the juicy black brambles. Some people say they are sour. Like us, these fruits become sweeter with sunshine. When they are ripe and shiny-black, they almost fall in your hands as you pick them. Today, looking at the numerous footsteps and flattened shrubs, I know a lot of us have received the gifts of the dunes while picking its wild fruits lately. Several mornings in a row I leave dressed in heavy raingear to defy the prickling bramble bushes and come back home, my basket filled to the brim with blackberrries, bramble or An dris bennaichte, botanically called the Rubus fruticosus.

Real blackberry lovers go for their fresh wake-up taste. In early summer the prickly plant, with its sometimes up to three metre long hanging and tangling branches, produces delicate white and pink flowers, like the rose family. August is their time for harvest, until Autumn Equinox.

I have my favourite 'vineyard' in the sandy soil of the Findhorn dunes. Where I thank and bless the Bramble Deva. With as much joy as I had as a teenage girl, when I picked my first bucket full of bramen in the Dutch dunes. My friend Heleen, and all her sisters and brothers and her mum and dad, all would get in the car loaded with buckets, pots and bags to Castricum aan Zee. To the Kennemerduinen, the dunes along the North Sea coast. The whole day we gathered and picked, only taking a break to eat our picnic of cheese sandwiches, coffee, and lemonade for us young ones.

It became a ritual, lasting now more than 40 autumns: end of August I go blackberry picking. In the footsteps of our ancestors, who gathered them as food thousands of years ago. Carefully collecting the ripe fruits. Cooking for jam. Pressing juice or making wine. Freezing the produce.

They top up my daily porridge. But they also give great taste and colour, fresh or cooked, in smoothies, puddings or ice creams.

The leaves can be dried or used fresh to make a tea. In times of no black tea, blackberry leaves were known as the best substitute. Four teaspoons full of dried or cut leaves in a teapot for a good infusion. Make it stronger as a gargle against throat and gum infections or diarrhoea. In Celtic times, rheumatism was believed to be cured by dragging the poor victim through the bramble bushes. If you'd like to try it…! In Scotland irritable people are called 'as cross as a bramble'; but know the bramble actually grows worldwide…

The druids saw the bramble with its tenacious roots as a symbol of holding your ground. I like that. Look at them, aren't they beautiful?

Findhorn, September 2010

Blackberrries in Findhorn dunes, 2011

Brambles (2)

A soon as I see her, my cheeks blush
I come nearer and
a wave of warmth surrounds me.
I am in love with my bramble!

She lies bathing in the autumn sunshine
Waiting for me? Smiling at me,
as if she knew I would come.
We had our portrait together taken today.
Look how we both glow!

And the next time
I'd like to lay myself next to her roots
and talk to her soul,
to get to know more her Self and her needs, and
her healing, nourishing gifts.

But, for today, I receive your last ripened fruits
blackening my fingers once again,
sweet sour on my tongue.
Love in my heart,
joy in my eyes.

It is Autumn Equinox.
We've had a lot of rain lately.
The air gets rough and raw
the wind tougher, coming from the sea
and the soil under our roots withdraws its warmth.
We're both changing
into the fall.

Findhorn, 26 September 2010   *Blackberrries in Findhorn dunes, 2014*

Holding the circle – the circle holding us

The large pebble found on the sandy Findhorn Beach holds a ring, an ellipse, a circle. It is one of the many beautiful patterns nature gives us. Ancient rock formations of different minerals fusing together. Amongst them granite, quartz, Lewisian Gneiss, sandstone, Time leaving its marks of ellipses and lines with which every pebble tells us its own story.

Our beach is full of stories.

Natural circles have been known since the beginning of time: the sun, moon, whirls in water or wind. They have been observed and have inspired our civilisation to develop geometry, astronomy and many inventions. We say that 'every circle is a magic circle', a sacred circle. In a circle of people coming together, an extra energy of spirit is present.

We draw a circle of protection. I remember once in the Sahara desert, while I was on a vision quest, drawing a large circle to mark my territory, creating a safe space. At home in the Findhorn community, we come together in a circle by holding hands to attune at the start and end of a gathering or job, or to bless the food.

And the circle is holding us.

Findhorn, 2012

Holding the Circle – The Circle Holding Us was part of a photo exhibition in the Universal Hall at Findhorn October-November 2011

Hands holding, 2009

Moving – We belong to the Earth

Let me start with the Earth. The song 'I feel the earth move under my feet' comes to mind. Although Carol King sang it as a love song to another human being, I sing my love to the Earth-being, Gaia, and today specifically to this part of the Earth at Findhorn village where I live. The 'castle' of Culbin Sands Apartments has hosted me for more than eight years. I love the views over the wide dune landscape filled with yellow gorse or purple heather. In bloom they are a colourful tapestry, drawing me in, to be at home in it. And I am. And I have been.

Being touched by the Earth
I feel touched while I touch the soft sand, the undulations of Gaia's skin on the beach, and I see I am built like Her, in Her image. I am soft, rough, uneven, broken, tough, delicate. This soil is calling me again and again. I am hers. In all weathers. How the very soil of a place binds us! First it calls us, the next thing it anchors us.

Earth does not seem to go together with change
Everything connected with the element earth seems to change very, very slowly. The movement within a rock or a mountain seems like nothing, doesn't it? Until it expresses itself in an earthquake, that's sudden, overwhelming. But everything is changing continuously. We know that, in theory. Small daily changes are easy to ignore, but they are signs we had better keep an eye on, to prepare ourselves for the big changes in our lives.

Moving house can be such a big change…
– I do not know yet! – even after I have moved house and country many times. The idea of having to leave my wonderful flat and maybe move from Findhorn is disturbing and inconvenient. I'll have to un-root. I will be uprooted and maybe even unsettled for a while, until I find a new home.

Through the process of moving I hope to learn some things:
like about homecoming in myself and improving how I adjust to the changes life brings. To stay in balance more easily, whatever is happening 'out there'. The spiritual teacher William Bloom, a regular visitor to Findhorn, once said: "Some people are not that sensitive to all the stimulus of the world around them, they are very earth-bound and calm." But, like William, I am not one of those people! So I'd like to listen more to the Goddess of the Earth, Tellus, Gaia or call her Terra Mater, to become her daughter. 'We belong to the Earth' and even if I might be a wandering daughter, having lived in many places on this planet, travelling for experience and gaining inner wisdom, I belong to this soil, to this part of the Earth called Findhorn.

Findhorn, 31 January 2015

Findhorn dunes with rabbit hole and view on Culbin Sands Apartments, 2008

The Earth is My Body

The Earth is my body
Water my blood
The Air is my breath
And Fire my spirit

I am singing this little song with a group of new arrivals during their Findhorn Experience Week. I am holding a nature sharing, like I have done so often over the last ten years. Every time is different though. I tell a bit about my experiences and ideas about Nature, and invite them to experience the creation or deepening of their own connection. For this we mostly go outside, sometimes in the dark, or even in the rain. We walk into the woods, to the top of one of the seven Cluny hills, to deeply breathe in the earthy smell of the soil, to breathe with the old trees, to touch with our skin the thick layers of fern, moss and decayed leaves and to let it touch us.

We humans so over-estimate our visual impressions (hear me say this as a photographer!) and however beautiful they are; when we close our eyes it is as if our other senses become more active. I gently kiss a young leaf bud, smilingly give it my love and in silence send it a message of encouragement. It can bring me to tears. Going into the woods is easier, but we don't have to do so to connect with what we call Nature. Wherever we are, actually we are not so much having a connection with Nature, as we are part of it. Many teachers nowadays remind us of this. We just need to become aware of it, feel it and live it.

With the rise of the scientific paradigm and Descartes' theories about dualism we started the belief that humanity was somehow separate from nature. This way of seeing the world was necessary to be able to conquer, control and damage the soil, the forests and pollute water and air.

There is no cell in my body though – take this skin, hair, bones or blood – that is literally not part of the Earth: it is made of this earth-stuff and as dust we will return to it, as it is written. It might be irrelevant, if we actually believe the proven science that in a former life we've been a rock, a bird or a tree, in other words if we made the evolution from minerals to animals to human beings. In a way, we, I, you, are this now. I am breathing in the air from the clouds above me, the very air the tree in my garden gives; I contain the calcium of the chalky rocks at our coast. The water of the river made up of rain and snow is the same as that which flows through my body.

It is said that on a spiritual level we are all One. Regularly I am challenged to take this in as my truth. Am I one with that nasty neighbour? With that murderer or that political dictator? That can't be true! ONLY if I acknowledge where in me I possess some of their qualities, however little or much, as author Debbie Ford writes, can I reach that belief. On the physical level we're also all One and for me this is easier to grasp, despite all our differences and uniqueness. We are built of the same earthy stuff. Thinking it through, layer after layer, I become aware I am that gorgeous fragrant reddish rose, you are that wonderful crucial cloud above us in the sky, we are our favourite tropical sandy beach … or that polluted sandy beach.

As there is no doubt anymore: we are in trouble. We are in the middle of a huge worldwide problem with our overpopulation, including a climatologic and extinction crisis and for thousands of species of plants and animals that die out each year it already is too late. Harming You (the Earth) is harming Me (Adriana). What a cruelty! So the practice is to be less masochistic? How can I stop hurting, damaging myself = Earth, in my everyday life?

I feel awareness is important. Love is important. Seeing, sensing the natural beauty that still is in and around us, protecting and caring for it, encouraging it and acting for it, might prove itself to be very, very helpful.

Not because we have to – however true this could be – but because we want to, from our heart.

April 2015

Findhorn Beach Pebble Project, 2009

A massive fire

Thinking of the Paasvuren, the Easter bonfires that are still made in the fields in the eastern Netherlands, I decided to make my own Paasvuur and, with the upcoming house move in mind, to burn my diaries. So I called my friend Annie to hear if she also was up for it. She was! At the edge of the sea and dunes of Findhorn, we sang, shouted and danced. I did a ritual to bless our past, with all its experiences of joy and pain, and release it with the old books as we threw and threw them into the fire. Our memories are enough.

Deep down inside me, an even bigger fire is burning. A huge fire of anger, outrage, grief, and also of compassion for the suffering. Its flames, spitting out tentacles, trying to claw at my energy, feed on me and overwhelm me.

It has been said that you can only mourn if you can love.

Once, during the preparation for a ritual at Findhorn to shed our tears for the suffering of the Earth, environmental activist Joanna Macy said: "It takes courage to fully live in a fear-phobic culture. The dominant system cannot tolerate the raw feelings of grief and anger about what has been done to our Earth". I'm sure it means the anger and fire in me, in you, cannot be seen as only our private pain – to deal with in hidden one to one therapeutic sessions – but as part of the collective (un) consciousness. The fire in me is for the ancient forests they've put to the flame to clear soil for cattle grazing. The fire in me is for the memory of being burned at the stake for the knowledge we had as women about the healing properties of plants, trees and stones; for the rituals we held to honour Mother Earth.

The fire in me is not a cosy barbecue or gas-lit fake wood-burning stove. I want to make a real fire to release my useless old, walk over the hot ashes, and burn away the skin, become raw alive again, renewed.

My fire is huge and it needs attention and to be tended by a real fire-woman.

Findhorn, March 2015

Cullerne Garden, 2011

The four directions

It has been said that it is in the East where Spirit lives, where the light is born. The place of inspiration and illumination. It has been said the East is the place of all new beginnings, of the new born, of the spring in the air. The colour of the East is yellow-gold.

She winked at me with a smile, inviting me to play, almost to be a child again. "I am the South," she whispered, and her spontaneity went under my skin, tickling, touching my senses, until we melted into the colour of red passion fruit and plum vine. I enjoy the energy of the South.

And it was in the West that my inner eyes opened to meet my own darkness. Here, in the West, is the place where our fears live, where our lessons lie. The place to connect with our ancestors and their gifts. To meet our own blues. And in this place of mystery, the West, we can find our destiny.

He says the North is the place where the words live. Where conflicts come from. Where wisdom can be obtained. He said the colour of the North is white. I think of snow and write down a list:
the frost
the winter
the cold
book-keeping (no, seriously!)
I acknowledge the North.

Findhorn, January 2008

Movement in Scotttish landscape, 2008

River Findhorn at Randolph's Leap, 2003

I am river

The river longing for the sea

The river flows towards the sea
Sometimes peaceful and calm
Sometimes outrageous and wild
But always powerful
Like the river longing for the ocean
Is my Self longing for Oneness

I am river

I am river
I see the sea
As I flow
And know
To go where
My heart belongs

The river mirroring my colourful being

The river is flowing and ever changing
Its shapes. Its colours. Its face.
It shapes, it colours, it faces.
Water powerfully reflects
And
The river is mirroring my own colourful being

The river taking me home

The river is flowing and flowing
Calm or wild but always powerful
Showing its true being
My true being
The river is taking me home to myself

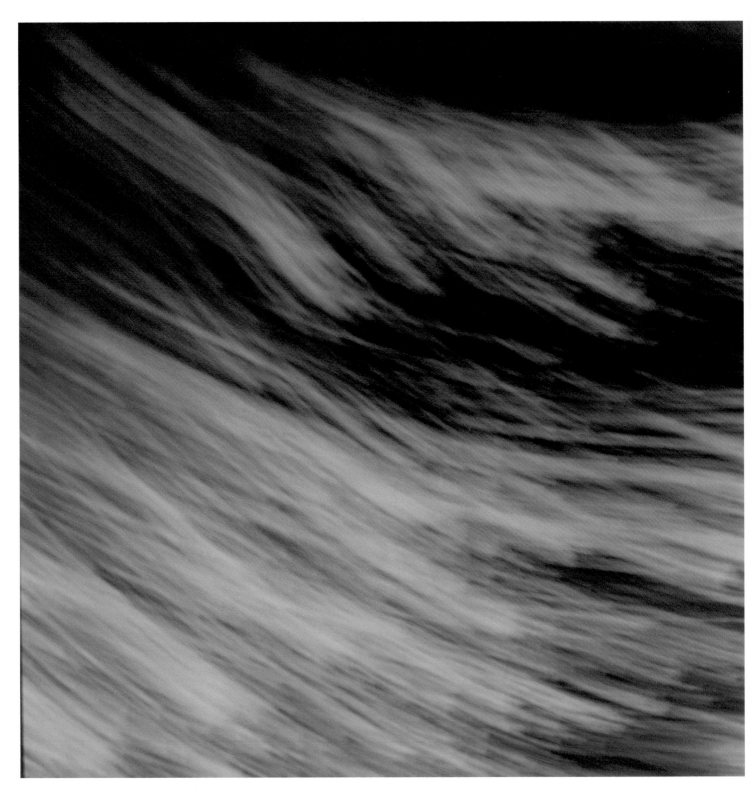

Once the wind wanted to be photographed

It was an extremely wild day. I looked out from a warm, cosy living room and in a flash I knew I had to make a photograph of the wind.

This turned out to be quite an adventure. It was storming fiercely and behind my house the trees swayed dangerously close to the windows of my darkroom. From inside it had looked wonderful, the trees, the bleak sunlight, but most of all the wind; it all looked like magic. As if I not only could hear it, but see it and even breathe with it. But I wanted more! I wanted to be with the wind.

So I picked up my medium-size Mamya camera (the double-eyed C220), put on a big weatherproof jacket to keep myself warm, and went outside.

And immediately from the patio into the open field corner, it was there. It hit me. Present in everything. I could sense it more and more with every step. I slowly stopped walking and leaned into or against it: held and, at the same time, pushed by the wind and its force. I closed my eyes and adjusted the camera on touch and slowly I was swayed like I had seen the trees doing earlier. The noise was deafening. What sound was coming from the trees? What was coming from the wind? What was from me, my own heavy breathing?

The gales inside me emerged until we merged: swaying, sweeping, storming – my hands out of my control directed and moved by the wind itself.

It was the wind who made this photo, I'm sure. A self-portrait by the wind.

Findhorn, August 2014

My love is

Pony horse at Cullerne Garden, 2010

Horses, cows and the healing power of animals

With their flowing manes they come to us through our myths and fairytales. Descendants of the Przewalksi wild horses from the steppes of central Asia were domesticated and welcomed humans onto their once wild backs. History was changed. A horse is seen as nobler than any other animal. A beautiful animal, true, as well as intelligent and faithful. Different, but for me not necessarily worth more than a panther, elephant or cow.

In my youth on a Dutch farm we had a heavy Belgian draught horse, before the tractors were introduced. We had sheep, chickens, sometimes goats, but most of all we had cows. Many cows with calves, young bulls and heifers. My parents started their dairy farm at the beginning of World War II with one cow my father had bought. A cow is not just a cow; there are many kinds. And they're not as stupid as we believe.

Anyway, our farm started with Hoekstra 5, one of those world famous black and white cattle breeds for milk production called Fries-Hollands. Generations of Hoekstras lived on the farm, until recently, when my retiring brother and sister-in-law ended the farm. Only after leaving home, did I get to know other cattle breeds, like the Dutch Lakenvelder and the Groninger Blaarkop (Groningen white headed cow) and then, in the 70s, as soon as the quota on milk production was introduced, foreign breeds for dual purpose (milk and beef production) were imported. Larger Holstein-Friesians, Italian meaty Piedmontese calves, the Limousin and beautiful white Blonde d'Aquitaine, both at home on French plains, and the Jersey cow. I like cows. Like cows, chickens or pigs, there are many horse breeds too. I'm just not familiar with them.

We hunt animals, eat them or have them as pets and companions in the home or farmstead. It makes me believe these animals made a commitment to be with people, even if we think we are the boss and owner.

The native American Indians as well as the Celtic druids said every person has a power or totem animal. Animals as symbols of healing power. Each animal shows us behaviour patterns in which we can discover healing messages; free for us to use. You don't 'horse around' with these powers. The white stallion brings the shield and power of wisdom and teaches that misuse of power never leads to wisdom.

 I think on my photo I actually show a Shetland pony, a horse of a small breed, grazing at Cullerne Gardens of Findhorn.

Findhorn, November 2014

Rain and more rain

And then the rains came

Sturdy sound on soil, receiving after being hardened off by sun, by wind, by cold again. The rains came and stayed with us for days. The highly pregnant clouds spilling over, filling over the rivers and the land, and my coat and shirt and trousers and pants, filling my skin and eyes. And then we cried together. And then we sang together

As the rains came.

It is right at the end of August. I would have liked to photograph the rain, which never seemed to stop falling here. From fine drizzles to pouring waves. We are in a part of the world (northern Scotland) where there is a bounty of water coming down, actually like some parts of India and South America, where rivers are flooding this August month. I did not see this on the news, but learned about it during my studies in (world) Spanish. One such flood was that of the immense Riachuelo-Matanza river-basin, which is said to be the most polluted in the world, and lies in a densely populated, industrial region, north of the Río de la Plata in Argentina. It worries me. Other parts of the world are suffering from drought. I think we are only just beginning to comprehend what climate change can actually do.

Later this year the United Nations will organise the Climate Change Conference 2015 in Paris. As Climate Central reports: "Even if the world manages to limit global warming to 2 degrees C – the target number for current climate negotiations – sea levels may still rise at least 6 metres (20 feet) above their current heights, radically reshaping the world's coastline and affecting millions in the process."* This is not good news. And will we cope? The reality might even be worse than all predictions, especially for the 'underdeveloped' and poor areas on our planet.

And it continues to rain outside.

Forres, September 2015

*Brian Kahn, 2015, Guardian Environmental Network, www.the guardian.com/environment/2015/july

Rain and storm at Randolph's Leap woods, 26 October 2008

Signs of summer

Signs of summer
Slowly appearing in the garden
Sensual
Radiant red
Ravishing Titian red
Rebellious red
Beetroot, blood and radishes,
Nevertheless sweet, as strawberries
Slowly appearing in the garden
With generosity, like the smile of a lover.
And a longing heart
Heated, redder than red, helpless suddenly
When She appeared in my garden.
Signs of summer
Bewildering peonies: the Paeoniaceae
Gorgeous poppies: the Papaverus orientalis and rhoeas
Zinging zestful zinnias: the Zinnea peruviana
To name but a few of them.

Forres, June 2015

Wild papaver orientalis, Findhorn, 2014

Flock of birds, Isle of Iona, 2014

Listening

The whole landscape is singing. There are so many sounds, not only from birds. Listen! These sounds are important for understanding the landscape we are in. Birds are calling to communicate and connect. Their songs are ancient, the Pleistocene still hanging in them. Then there are the winds. Whirling and lying down like high and low tides.

The birds are aware of the wind. They avoid, connect, and use it to make their journeys, to play, to show off or to simply be bird. But is the wind aware of the birds, does it hear their songs? And is the wind feeling me, like I feel the wind? Is the sensual touch and warmth mutual? And does it matter to the wind what it connects with, I wonder. Like when it clashes into an old shed and blows it over or whenever it confronts an old missus struggling on her bike to come home; does it matter to the wind if it plays or destroys? I would like to know. I would like to know if you feel my gratitude, dear wind, whenever I feel your caress on my skin and I deeply inhale you into my lungs; which then helps me to open my heart, leaving my body shaking and in love with you. I would like to share this together. It does me good to believe you do notice and that my energy, my aura, also touches you. As then I will be wind like you are. Air. Energy.

Suddenly I smell something. The wind actually brings along to my nostrils a strong acid smell of animal manure.

Or have I just been talking bullshit?

May 2008/ May 2016

Quam Pulchra Es

Every Sunday morning, Findhorn sings Taizé. The French community of Taizé is a Christian singing community. For me those songs are much too associated with suffering as a noble life purpose, as taught by the nuns and priests at my girls' primary school. Too many patriarchal Lords and 'De Heer' and holy men in heaven for me. I had turned my back to Catholicism in my teenage years. They had tried to keep us, youngsters at the end of the 60s, in the church by introducing a rhythmic service on Saturday nights, which we called the 'beatmis' (beat-mass), with guitars and songs in Dutch instead of in Latin. In vain. In whatever language, no reason to promote misery. For me in my teenage years, it seemed real life was filled with enough of it. So I only visited the church at funerals, of which I also had too many for my age.

Now decades later, life looks different. I love to sing and dance together. Different from Taizé, I prefer the songs from the many other traditions from around the world that we sing at Findhorn. Simple circle dances and live music accompany some of the songs. It is a highlight in my week and nowadays I go whenever I have enough energy, after the early nine o'clock healing meditation in the main sanctuary. It feels like a community coming together, a spiritual social event at The Park.

Last Sunday we sung the old Latin song from the book of Solomon, Quam Pulchra Es: how beautiful you are, my beloved friend. My voice breaks halfway in emotion. I love the song and would love to hear it at my own funeral, I think. For all of us humans, eternal beings. I sing it for you and hope you can sing it for me, now and then.

The song brings me back to my early youth and I faintly hear the singing of the tall men in black suits carrying the coffin on the path along the Roman Catholic Church, along the endless churchyard under the high poplar trees, noisy in the wind with black crows. The same voices of the male choir high at the balcony of the church on Sunday's Latin High Mass.

On we continue with a passionate South-American song, Altísimo Corazón. Hear the guitar. Imagine the castanets. We sing and then we dance and wildly swirl together in a celebration of life and love. Let's fill our glasses and toast to the abundance and beauty on our planet. It's an honour to be part of it, of our common evolution.

Findhorn, 8 March 2016

My love since 1997: tree at Magic Triangle,
near Cullerne Garden, later part of West Whins, 2014

Heather

Purple plots on the sandy dunes attract my attention. I'd like to touch them, stroke them as you do a velvet cushion waiting for you. I'd like to lie down on them and then disappear in between their abundance of little purple flowers. Heather it is called, like my friend Heather. Erica is its botanical name. There is a village in the former lower-moorland colonies of the east Netherlands given the name Erica by its first settlers. They found endless purple meadows of this low growing vegetation on the peaty soil they came to excavate.

Erica, the name brings up images of sweet women with live, lasting love, of truth, faithfulness and honesty.

Well we are just into July and the heather in the Findhorn dunes is expanding from the earth. Suddenly its purple colour appears in the normally dull brownish low shrubs. Firmly rooted in the soil, or on hilly bulges. I even found one big plant uprooted, and hanging totally upside down, while it continued to grow. To be able to admire it, I also had to radically change position. Lying down flat on the sandy soil, I could photograph it, watching this phenomenon in awe. It had a lesson for me: however upside down my life looks like, I just have to be with it, accept it and keep on growing!

I remember strong winds blowing over the moorlands. Centuries of loneliness. Carts with creaking wheels and the ox walking in front of us to collect the harvest from the yellow weaving buckwheat fields. Long trudges along the wooden paths laid over the wetland, to reach the grain mill of the monastery, where the monks sell the flour for our bread. Fertility. Fragrance of promise.

This afternoon I will take a nap in the dunes, as I like to do. The sun is high, the light bright. I'll lay my head resting on Erica's petals and doze away, dreaming of harvest dance feasts in the barns. After the rich harvest. I'll hear the violin and the accordion playing. I'll listen to the clear sound of an alto voice, dark from the dust of the day and of beer flowing. Maybe I'll dance with her later on, when the musicians take over again and she'll be free to twirl and twiddle with me on the ongoing jolly tunes. We'll wear wreaths made with daisies and Erica in our hair and we'll smell of hay and sweat and sweet laughter. Round and round we'll go.

Findhorn, 2008

Heather in Findhorn dunes, 2008

Lady Dahlia

Lady Dahlia. Don't be fooled by the lady Dahlia. Her outer petals may have begun to fade, but underneath her fulsome petal petticoat is still arrayed in radiant colours. A dying dahlia bloom droops limply from her stem. I raise her face to mine like the tilting of a chin. I lay her down upon my palm.

She opens

Pulsing like a heart

A heart beat

She breathes and opens once again.

Findhorn, around 2003/4

Dahlia, 2005

Tulips

The famous Dutch painter Judith Leyster lived in Haarlem in the Dutch Golden Age, the 17th century. She became the first female Master painter and had, like her colleague Frans Hals, a studio and students. Quite some of her work long was believed to be of the hand of Frans Hals. To my surprise I once found myself in tears in front of the original oil painting of her self-portrait, made around 1630, hanging in the Frans Hals Museum, in the picturesque ancient street Klein Heiligland in Haarlem. Since I discovered her during my art education in the early eighties, I always loved her work. It radiates self-confidence and joie de vivre. She inspires me four centuries after she died.

As well as her famous oil portraits, she painted tulips, lots of tulips, on paper. Her tulip books became very popular and became the first visual catalogues for tulip traders during the Tulpomania investment speculation that hit the Netherlands and made the bourse crash in 1635.

Haarlem still lies in the middle of a tulip area. I have great memories of living in that town on the river Spaarne during several episodes of my life. Think of the Netherlands and many people automatically think of tulips, so the famous Keukenhof flower show made 'Holland' their theme this year.

Amidst all the flowers I have photographed, tulips have their own unique place, as I always loved them. I created this image to honour the tulip and Judith Leyster.

Findhorn, April 2014

Painting tulips, Netherlands, 1989

Get to know the real Stars…

There is more to this Christmas Star flower than meets the eye. You might know the Poinsettia (Euphorbia pulcherrima) as a cheery houseplant which flowers around Christmas and reaches around 30-40 cm. This little plant is actually a shrub, originally from Mexico, and in the tropics can grow up to four meters.

What a presence it has! I was surprised and overjoyed to meet some of these tree-like beauties earlier this month when I was visiting La Gomera, one of the Canary Islands. Its large green leaves slowly, wonderfully change into an overwhelming feast of bright red and orange flowers. It receives the light. It allows the light. This reminds me of Winter Solstice, when we, after some dark months here up in the north, are quite ready for the turning of the sun and receiving its light again; the rebirth of the Sun. Like the Poinsettia we dance to the Light.

The Mother (of Auroville in India) received the following, as guidance from the over-lighting being of the Poinsettia: "Opening of the vital to the Divine love – little by little it is no longer the ego that governs, but the Divine." Read it again. I need some practice to bring this into my life. How about you?

What stays with me, apart from the plant's beautiful colours, is this 'allowing the light in'. Allowing ourselves to be as big and beautiful and bold as we are. Let us. Happy Solstice, Christmas and New Year.

Findhorn, December 2014

Pointisettia, Findhorn,2014

The Green Alkanet is conquering The Park

Don't worry though, the Green Alkanet is not a kind of Pictish knight (imagine one played by Mr Bean in the movie version). It is simply a plant. A wild plant, which, despite its name, flowers in blue. The green alkanet. Botanically called the Pentaglottis sempervirens (the five-tongued ever-turning one?) of the borage family. No, not speedwell, nor flax. I've never seen a green variety of the green alkanet, have you? So, there still is a question about its genes, its ancestry or heritage to be solved.

Clouds of blue appear along the paths in The Park. Not a timid personality. It likes to arrive in abundance. Upright. Bristly. Bees love these flowers. I am quite fascinated by the bright coloured, five-petalled small flowers arranged on the tall hairy stems. I let them more or less take over the tiny garden I should weed. Green alkanet claims soil place, but is not a real nutrient robber, like some of its colleagues. Take the wild red poppy (Papaver rhoeas). However fabulous they look in your garden, all your other plants will soon need iron infusions, as the poppy will have sucked it all up. Better also avoid, if I may give some advice here, letting the Indian balsam (Impatience glandulifera) pop its seeds all around the place later this summer. If it does, like an agricultural monoculture, nothing else will grow there next year, or maybe only the giant hogweed as companion. Surely they are impressive, but if you like to go for BIG in your garden, try the various perennial Angelica species (of the carrot family). Its white, robust, domed umbels, can reach up to two metres. Or plant some fennel (Foeniculum vulgare) and embrace its sea of feathery green, luminous yellow and fresh fragrance. Mmhhh.

And it will triumph over the green alkanet.

Wild flowers growing at roadsides, their seeds travelling around to uncontrolled spaces, they seem eternal. Of all times, and as such, the above mentioned alkanet, and all other wild flowers, including cow parsley, cuckoo flower, meadow buttercup and hedge bindweed are flowers of my youth. All now-cultivated flowers once were growing wild. Travelling independently, or brought to new places, where they are no longer in native soil, but still retain the imprint of their growth habit and their original seasons. Resilient to changed circumstances. Like snowdrops flowering in our winter snow. Like the Poinsettia, at their best in bright red blossom with our Christmas, when it is high summer in their homes in the tropics. Memories stored in their genes. Every seed, every bud, still remembers.

Probably every cell in our human bodies also holds stored memory; long forgotten by ourselves. Which youth traumas, stresses and sins of young adulthood do they express now, decades later in an alarming distress we call illness? The cells speak, in my case loud as a scream, conquering other healthy cells, but I don't seem to understand their language. However much I listen. Their sounds so foreign. Their signs so unfamiliar. As if they do not come from my own cells nor my history, but from somewhere else. From something much larger.

Findhorn/ Elgin, May/August 2016

Green alkanet, Findhorn

Loving Lupins

The first things that caught my eye at my new accommodation were the lupins. Majestical and noble, they were standing guard at the entrance of the path up to the house. Although their spines looked very straight, they were far from stiff, with their delicate, pea-like flowers growing in dense whorls around a tall spike in a soft apricot abundance. 'Welcome!' they waved to me as I entered further, and was pleasantly distracted by a group of bright red Papaver orientalis surrounded by at least five different colours of aquilegias. "This looks good!" I exclaimed. "I like this little garden." There was another group of the Lupinus in the same soft yellowish-orange colouring.

It draws my mind back to the farm where I grew up. Back to some sweet tender memories. My mother must have loved lupins to bits, as our ornamental garden contained seas of them, in cadmium orange and crimson, in lavender, lilac and purple, in plum and pink and reds of all shades. I totally loved them too. After her early death, my father told me to choose the seeds for our flower gardens. Lupins, though, were never seen again there; my father did not allow it. The reason was, he told me, mumbling, that he just did not like them. But I missed them, as I missed her, and the gardens never were the same again.

The owner of my new temporary home, at the moment in Canada, immediately recognised the herbaceous perennial plant on the photo I sent. Last year his woman friend had taken some of its seeds – which come in a pod as fruit– to sow in her own Canadian garden. Two gardens, two people on different sides of the earth, connected by lupins and love. Most likely they grow very well there.

There are many species of the Lupinus albus and perennis, and they grow everywhere in Europe. For thousands of years they have been found around the Mediterranean, as well as in North and South America, where, it has been discovered, especially in the Andes, the legume seeds or beans have been grown for food for 6000 years. From my agricultural years in the Netherlands, I remember that farmers grow them as green manure, to nourish the soil. A meadow full of these yellowish flowers looks astonishing. Nowadays the lupin bean is increasingly popular as food again, as a healthier alternative to soya beans. Full of protein. An antioxidant and a prebiotic. And gluten free!

I would start to grow them in my veggie patch right away. Lupins. And more lupins. Partly to nourish and heal the body, partly as an ornamental flower to heal my heart and to brighten my days.

Now bring me that garden! As that is still missing. With a house, my long-term home to be. Yes, please.

Kinloss, 9 June 2016

Lupins, 2016,
Kinloss

Seven flowers from Cullerne Garden

These seven little flower texts were written in 2003/4 to celebrate life, and Cullerne Garden. Cullerne Garden was my work department, both as trainee and staff, at the Findhorn Foundation Community from spring 1998 until spring 2006. In my work there as a gardener and also as a photographer, I grew into a deep appreciation of the garden, and all its visible and invisible helpers. And especially of the flowers. I have been blessed enough to meet them in their essence, to take care of them and help them grow, while they, in turn, helped me to grow.

Papaver orientalis

Most poppies that grow in the garden are self-seeded, emerging each year unaided by the gardeners, surprising us every time with their variations in colour and shape. Look at the Rhoeas in fiery red, in bright pink, in lilac. And what about the huge wild Orientalis, which always chooses a view on the vegetable fields? They cry for passion to come alive, to be visible. They are! Are we? Do we dare?

The poppy's greyish-black centre hides a large collection box. When the box is dry, it will use the winds to shake out and spread around an abundance of tiny black seeds. Variations of this seed are also used on the famous Park Kitchen poppy cake, a delicious dessert served for celebrations at the Findhorn Foundation.

Lathyrus odoratus

The favourites of many gardeners and guests. So very English. And sweet. We grow the sweetpea against our old barn, so that we can enjoy them during our tea breaks nearby. Tea breaks become a delight. Harvesting them becomes a celebration, surrendering and indulging in their fragrance, leaving us lightly in love with everything. By then, we have already been through the joyous process of choosing which varieties to grow this year; the skill of sowing, pricking out, pinching, potting and staking … and feeding, yes, lots of feeding. The sweetpeas receive our seaweed and nettle compost manure, and lots of nourishing mulch.

Calendula officinalis

Scottish marigold. Dear calendula, how can we praise you enough? For your simplicity and your easy growing, being resistant to Scottish winters. You are a fantastic companion plant in organic farming; in the poly tunnels, you do such good work collecting aphids. Providing a nice herbal tea, edible too, making a great show on our salads. You are a beautiful, bright, cut flower, lighting up our flower bunches from spring 'til autumn. I like your funny curly seeds and attractive petals. Used in flower essences, you actually are one of the most well-known healing flowers for medical use. Thank you for all your gifts.

Dahlia

These were the first flowers I met in Cullerne Garden in spring 1998, and they became my darlings. They encouraged me to stay in Findhorn! Dahlias were also the flowers of my youth on a farm in the Netherlands, and I remember our house being filled with them. Now Cullerne is full of them. For most people it is 'all or nothing' with the dahlia.

This flower is my easiest entrance to the Overlighting Being and the Divine. I meditate with them. I sing and sit with them. I consult them to find out if they want to stay in the cold ground or if we have to take them out before winter arrives – they are not frost resistant – and every year their answer is absolutely right, of course. They teach about grounding love. They talk about the unlived dreams of our youth.

continued on next page

Paeonia

The peonies' beauty is about abundance. They live in the ornamental garden at Cullerne House, now part of Findhorn Flower Essences. Together with the large, strong sycamore tree, they are the eye catchers in that part of the garden. The peonies and the sycamore seem like opposites, yet both share the quality visibility. The peony takes your breath away when opening its core:
Soft
Gentle
Vulnerable
Beautiful.

Viola

The wild variety of this small violet, the Viola tricolore, known as heartsease, is used for its healing qualities. We sometimes pick them fresh for our garden herbal tea. Its larger sister, the pansy, likes borders, the heartsease mostly lives on edges of and in between the rows of cutting flowers. They seem to connect with others so easily. Don't they look full of compassion, as if they themselves can hold our tears? In the 1970s, the Deva of this flower gave this message to community co-founder Dorothy Maclean: "You find in us a power and authority as great as that of the large trees, although we are the smallest flower you have contacted."

Chrysanthemum tricolore

The people doing the gardening at Findhorn are often beginners, and so it is nice to have some reliable flower plants. This annual late summer flower is one such flower, and yet it can also surprise us. I just love the unexpected colour of the tricolore, as well as its robust fragrance. She calls us to be with her, to really see her and to open our hearts. And to me, when I first photographed her and let her be star of my pictures … I melted and lost myself in her. And still do. She reminds me of one guidance of The Beloved to Eileen (Caddy): "You are surrounded by Beauty everywhere. Have I not told you many times that which is within is reflected without?" Thank you flower, thank you Divine, for telling us, showing us, again and again.

Findhorn, 2003/4

Quotations used by kind permission of Dorothy Maclean and Eileen Caddy.

Heaunes, 2008

First Edidtion 2018

Text editor: Catharine Stott, catharinesott@yandex.com
Proof reading and corrections: Pat Ellison

The family and publisher have compiled this publication with great care, and to the best of their knowledge, in order to keep the intellectual legacy of Adriana Sjan Bijman alive.

Family and publisher cannot be held liable for any damage, whatever its nature, resulting from decisions based on the information in this book.

Print production by Big Sky Print, Findhorn. Printed with vegetable oil-based ink on FSC mix credit paper

ISBN number: 978-1-78926-066-3 Light scribbles from a nomad heart